AMERICAN CARNAGE

N

Nation Books

Nation Books is a collaboration between *The Nation* magazine and OR Books.

The Nation was founded by abolitionists in 1865 and still appears quarterly in print and online at thenation.com.

OR Books is a publishing company that embraces progressive change in politics, culture, and the way we do business. Find out more at orbooks.com.

Also available from Nation Books

The Nine Have Spoken

The Nation vs. the Supreme Court, 1870 to Today

Edited by Richard Kreitner

Forthcoming in this series

The Myth of Red Texas

How Reclaiming Our State's Radical Tradition Can Help Us Beat The Right

By David Griscom

Obsolete

Power, Profit, And The Race For Machine Superintelligence

By Garrison Lovely

The Great Betrayal

How the Democrats Became the Party of War

By James Carden

Against Black Nationalism

From Pan-Africanism to the New Deal

By Paul Prescod

American Carnage follows eleven federal workers, in eight government agencies, from the time they were told they were fired in the early weeks of Donald Trump's second presidential administration through to the summer of 2025. With Trump having empowered the world's richest man, Elon Musk, and his Department of Government Efficiency, to make dramatic cuts to many of the country's most important agencies, what unfolded in these months was a cascading tragedy of historic proportions.

Their stories, which show a country in a profound moment of crisis and dislocation, are America's stories. What happened to them—the bullying, the intimidation, the deliberate removal of financial stability—also happened to hundreds of thousands of other employees. A fierce reckoning with the intimate and far-reaching effects of these layoffs, both on the individuals who lost their jobs and on the millions of Americans who found their access to basic government services curtailed, *American Carnage* is the first book-length account of how these cuts dulled and denuded our city on the hill, leaving a morally impoverished landscape in their wake.

AMERICAN CARNAGE

HOW TRUMP, MUSK, AND DOGE
BUTCHERED THE US GOVERNMENT

SASHA ABRAMSKY

N

Nation Books

Published in association with OR Books

First printing 2025

The manufacturer's authorised representative in the EU for
product safety is Authorised Rep Compliance Ltd, 71 Lower
Baggot Street, Dublin D02 P593 Ireland (www.arccompliance.com)

Typeset by Lapiz Digital. Printed by BookMobile, USA, and CPI, UK.

paperback ISBN 978-1-68219-676-2
ebook ISBN 978-1-68219-662-5

DEDICATION:

To the men and women who labor each day to make the world a slightly better place, and who too often do not get the recognition they deserve.

and to my family, who give me so many reasons to care.

"He pronounced him the greatest of all imposters, who, possessed of no valuable qualifications, should deceive men by representing himself capable of governing his country... He also said that the man was equally void of sense, who, though he knew nothing, thought that he would seem good for something because of his riches, and though evidently despicable, would gain esteem."

—Xenophon's *Memorabilia of Socrates*

PROLOGUE

Ever since her father had taken her to his place of work at the National Institute for Occupational Safety and Health (NIOSH), Hannah Echt had always wanted to work there. Other kids dreamed of being astronauts or firefighters; Echt desired nothing more than to be an industrial hygienist, investigating dangerous workplace conditions and coming up with solutions that would help save workers' lives. As a young adult, she realized that dream, conducting workplace evaluations at places as diverse as railyards, construction sites, and cannabis processing facilities. Then, in early 2025, everything ground to a sudden halt. Following Donald Trump's January inauguration and DOGE's onslaught against federal employees, her Cincinnati office's "funds were frozen, travel was paused, and external communications, including our ability to publish and present our findings, were stifled." Months later, large parts of the NIOSH operations were still non-functional.

By the spring of 2025, the deliberately manufactured dysfunction was encroaching into pretty much every corner of the federal government. "It's made me doubt myself," Carmen Drier (not their real name), a probationary employee at the US Geological Survey who was fired and then, in the wake of court orders, begrudgingly rehired, admitted. "It just played into my fears and jerked me around for no good reason." Drier, who is nonbinary and uses "they/them" pronouns — an act of defiance in the face of federal orders to remove pronouns from the signature lines of government emails — worried that they weren't equipped with the skills needed to succeed in life. After all, this was their first job out of college, and now the government was making it clear it wanted to fire them. They worried that their performance on the job wasn't good enough. In their office, the pessimism as winter gave way to spring was contagious. Each morning, colleagues commuted to work in a funk, girding themselves for the next onslaught. "There's such anger and bitterness," Drier observed. "Everyone's trying their best to keep their cool, but every morning is just a sullen time. You're being told [by the government] that what you do is worthless."

At the Consumer Financial Protection Bureau, workers were bombarded with one extraordinarily demeaning email after another. On February 8, they were directed to "halt several classes of work unless 'required by law' or expressly approved by the Acting Director." They were ordered by that acting director to "cease any pending investigations" and not to open any new ones; to "cease all supervision and examination activity," and to "cease all stakeholder engagement." In short, they were mandated to stop doing everything that their agency had been created to do. Two days later, the acting director followed up by telling the CFPB staff that the headquarters building they worked in was closed and that "employees should not come into the office. Please do not perform any work tasks... employees should stand down from performing any work task." But eighteen days later, having been told that they couldn't work they were then ordered to fill in the Musk-mandated questionnaire listing "5 bullets describing what you accomplished last week and cc your manager. Going forward, please complete the above task each week by Mondays at 11.59pmET." It was, quite simply, Orwellian: having been ordered not to carry out their duties, or even to show up to their place of work, they were now being forced to justify their continued employment by saying what work accomplishments they had achieved each week.

* * *

The book that you are now reading follows eleven federal workers from the time they were told they were fired in the early weeks of Donald J. Trump's second presidential administration through to the summer of 2025. Some were comfortable with their names being used. Others were terrified of retribution and would talk only on condition that their names and other identifying characteristics were shielded. Some reacted to being fired by curling up in bed and crying; others binged on pizza; still others exercised obsessively. Some became paralyzed by indecision, others leapt into fix-it mode. They reacted, in short, in the myriad ways that millions of other Americans would react in the face of traumatizing, and potentially financially devastating, events.

Their stories are America's stories. What happened to them — the bullying, the intimidation, the denigration of character, and the deliberate removal of financial stability — also happened to hundreds of thousands of other employees. And the destruction wrought on the institutions they worked at was mirrored by similar scenes of carnage throughout the federal government, and in non-profits and universities reliant on federal grant money, as the Administration took a chainsaw to everything from disease prevention to basic environmental research, from pre-school programs and enforcement of civil rights laws to crime victims' services and food safety inspections. The pain they felt is one mirrored by the pain — and the shock — experienced by people in the US denied access to services once taken for granted, as retirees stand in line for hours at under-staffed Social Security offices to try to access benefits they have paid into their entire working lives; as consumers cheated by large financial institutions realize they no longer have advocates in their corner in the federal government; as survivors of the World Trade Center attacks have their healthcare services curtailed; as veterans are denied access to mental health and substance abuse services; as the homeless find even fewer federal resources directed their way. So too, it is a pain felt by desperately impoverished men, women, and children overseas whose lives were once made better, even if just at the margins, by organizations such as USAID, and who now are left having to find ways to survive in a landscape from which America has decided to absent itself.

As I reported this book, I realized that I was getting an inside view on one of the most extraordinary episodes in American political history. The stories that *American Carnage* chronicles collectively paint a picture of a country in a profound moment of crisis and dislocation. In the opening months of 2025, a year as consequential to American politics and society as any since the early days of the New Deal, the federal government's social contract with its workers to provide good, stable, conditions of employment, and with the population to provide core social services, was breaking down.

The implications of this breached social contract are stark: a younger generation of would-be public sector employees is being scared off of government work, and the American populace as a whole is facing a new reality in which everything from the ability to enroll in Social Security to the ability to get public health information from the CDC is being corroded.

* * *

Amid all of the rolling chaos and political upheaval of 2025, the Donald Trump-Elon Musk attack on federal employees and on the structures of the civil service system, enacted via the machinations of Musk's shadowy so-called Department of Government Efficiency — DOGE — stands out for its cruelty and also for its destruction of basic government functions.

Within days of DOGE's engineers, many of them barely out of their teens and with little to no knowledge of how complex government bureaucracies and programs operated, having been set loose on the American government, a cascade of cuts flowed through Washington, DC, and onto points beyond. The constitution be damned, Musk's team was on a mission to simply "delete" Congressionally-mandated programs they deemed wasteful and institutions they felt were antithetical to the values of the MAGA movement. In this frenetic assault on government function, tens of thousands of ordinary workers became collateral damage.

For some, that meant losing jobs they had moved across the country to take on; for others, further into their federal careers, it meant an implosion of retirement dreams — a fired federal worker with less than twenty years of service, and a lower civil service rank, gets a far more basic pension than they would have had they been allowed to work a few more years.

One of the women whose story is detailed in this book was an Atlanta-based CDC communications specialist who was subjected first to being fired as a probationary worker, then — after she had been rehired under court order — to being fired again as part of a broader Reduction-In-Force mandate. In meetings she attended during those brief weeks she had been rehired, her colleagues kept breaking down in tears. "By the time I was fired on February 14, I was already exhausted by what the administration was putting government employees through, and it hadn't even been a month," she recalled. As the year progressed and her anxiety about her family's financial situation intensified, she had to have hard conversations with her husband about whether they could afford to continue to keep their son in daycare and whether they should postpone the decision to have a second child. A scientist who had been booted out of the National Oceanic and Atmospheric Administration and, in the process, been cut off from her health insurance, was having to ration her last remaining doses of the medication she needed to keep her Crohn's Disease in check. A twenty-year Navy vet who had lost his job with the Forest Service was having conversations with his partner about calling it a day in the US and moving overseas. A long-time employee of the National Oceanic and Atmospheric Administration had concluded that the federal government could no longer be trusted as an employer. "I have no intention of ever returning to Federal service," he declared, "and will forever look back to this chapter as a shitshow of the highest order."

One after another, federal workers told me they were struggling to sleep, were wracked with anxiety, and found themselves fighting more often with their partners. Some had begun taking anti-depressants, or medications used to treat PTSD, to counter the dread they felt surrounding their work; others couldn't handle the emotional roller coaster of not knowing from one day to the next whether they were still employed and, despite believing their jobs provided important services to the American public, opted instead for Musk's Fork In The Road, taking deferred resignation offers or signing up for early retirement.

None of this cruelty was incidental; rather, it was the main point. The federal government, the largest employer in the country, had decided that its workers were the enemy within. Indeed, Russell Vought, architect of Project 2025 and Trump's choice to head up the Office of Management and Budget, was on record as saying he wanted federal employees to be "traumatically affected." A month before the election, *ProPublica* had released a video recording of Vought saying of the workers, "when they wake up in the morning, we want them to not want to go to work, because they are increasingly viewed as the villains. We want their funding to be shut down... We want to put them in trauma." Now, the administration was setting out to do just that.

"It's going to leave a black mark on my federal record of employment. Every time something happens to a federal employee, there's a form called a Notification of Personnel Action, an SF 50. When you apply for a federal job, you have to give in your most recent SF 50. And mine says 'terminated,'" said Kelsey

Hendrix, a blind woman who was fired from her job as a procurement and contracts specialist with NOAA. "That's the first thing a human resources manager will see when I apply for a new job." She worried that even in the private sector the termination notice would hinder her ability to find new work; that, in their hurry to find excuses to fire people, the DOGE-enforcers had conjured up a fictitious "poor performance" rationale that would haunt her for the rest of her career. It was, she said, an "unimaginably cruel" thing to do.

On a near-daily basis, Musk — whose personal fortune was so gargantuan that he could have paid the *entire* federal workforce, of 2.3 million people, for a year, and covered for all of their work-related benefits as well, and still been left with more than $100 billion in assets — amped up the pressure. He tweeted out to his more than 200 million followers pronouncements about which agencies would bite the dust next. He declared that USAID was a "criminal organization," and that it was "time for it to die." Then, when his engineers began dismantling it, firing its staff and refusing to pay its overseas contractors, he gloated that he had spent the weekend feeding the agency into a woodchipper. The world's richest man promised to "delete" the Consumer Financial Protection Bureau, and, once the mass firings at the organization started, mocked it by tweeting out RIP to the CFPB.

At Musk's behest, agencies imposed onerous new restrictions on employees, as well as make-work tasks seemingly designed for the sole purpose of tormenting workers and hounding them out of their positions. All federal employees were ordered to send a weekly email detailing five things they had done the previous week that would justify their continued employment. Their work credit cards were either canceled or limited to being able to spend a mere one dollar a day on them. Most work-related travel was eliminated. Office buildings were sold off. Remote workers were ordered to return to in-person work only to find buildings with non-functional toilets, offices with no furniture, heating, and air-conditioning systems that had been turned off, and so on.

For those who didn't get the hint, letters soon went out telling thousands upon thousands of workers that their services were no longer needed by the government. They were ordered to clear their desks and hand in their cell phones and computers and workplace IDs. In many instances, they were frog-marched out of the buildings they had worked in and unceremoniously deposited on the streets outside. All that was missing was a kick in the rear-end to complete the picture.

* * *

This was the hallmark of the opening act of Trump's second presidency. It was ruthless and cruel, with humiliation a core tactic to bring perceived enemy institutions and individuals to their knees.

Having been twice impeached as a result of actions during his first presidency, and having faced years of criminal indictments and trials, as well as civil lawsuits, the president was on a wrecking mission. He had, a year earlier, promised to be his supporters' sword of justice and their retribution; now he sought to make that a reality, to burn to the ground a system he viewed as having cheated and harassed and attempted to imprison him, and that his supporters viewed as being hopelessly entangled in a globalist vision they no longer wanted a part of. In 2025, he seemed intent on knee-capping the federal government and breaking beyond repair many of the agencies and funding systems that enabled ordinary citizens to access government services and benefit from government research.

Bolstered by a Supreme Court ruling that presidents were largely immune from criminal liability for any actions they could plausibly declare to be done in the official line of duty — which in practice covered pretty much everything — as well as by the realization from his previous go-around in the White House that the threat of impeachment by the House followed by conviction by the Senate was a paper tiger, he set out in the days and weeks after his inauguration to bypass Congress in fundamental decision-making, to ignore unfavorable court rulings and to eviscerate basic constitutional principles. In his sights were disparate groups: immigrants, law firms, universities, non-profits, journalists, democracy advocates at home and overseas, as well as ex-officials — in the Department of Justice, the military, in public health agencies, in regulatory offices, and in Ombudsmen roles — against whom he held a personal grudge. Most spectacularly, he had decided to target basic institutional pillars upholding the constitutional system of governance that had defined the United States since its founding, as well as the professional civil service that had developed, as a reaction against a previous era of corruption, from the late nineteenth century onward. Trump wanted to take a sledgehammer to the federal bureaucracy in a way that would make it practically impossible to resurrect; he desired to destroy entire agencies and departments, to fire hundreds of thousands of workers, and to do so entirely without Congressional buy-in. This was a full flowering of the charismatic Will to Power that America had never before witnessed.

In this nihilistic vision, imported wholesale from the hard-right Project 2025 manifesto, and with more than a passing similarity to the governing style of overseas autocrats such as Vladmir Putin, in Russia, and Viktor Orban, in Hungary, there wouldn't be hearings and there wouldn't be laws passed; there wouldn't be actions taken by Congress to revoke previously voted-on acts creating these agencies, or previously voted-on budgets funding these agencies — both of which are, constitutionally, within Congress's purview. Instead, Trump would usurp these powers, essentially ruling by decree; and he would appoint Elon Musk, the wealthiest man on earth, to run the shadowy new DOGE organization, which would do an end-run around the Constitutionally mandated separation of powers. In the ruthless opening act of Trump 2.0, Musk's teams, at times backed up by armed US marshals, would secure access to the financial and information pipelines that kept both information and funds flowing around the government, from government agencies to tens of millions of individual Americans, and also out to myriad organizations dotted around the country and the world.

What followed was, metaphorically at least, a slaughter.

The breadth of the proposed destruction was extraordinary. Services provided by the Department of Veterans Affairs to disabled veterans were being terminated; health centers in deeply conservative rural regions were being shuttered; Social Security Administration personnel were being fired, making it harder for people to enroll in Social Security; cancer research was being eviscerated; units that diagnosed everything from drug-resistant STDs through to TB and hepatitis were terminated; specialized anti-corruption teams at the Department of Justice were let go; programs that worked with survivors of the World Trade Center attack were defunded. Each day, new cuts were announced; each day, additional tranches of federal employees found they no longer had jobs.

Here, in 2025, was a genuine explosion of American Carnage, the specter that Trump, in his bleak 2017 inauguration speech, had warned was stalking the country. It was being inflicted on the US not by overseas foes, not by terrorist organizations, not by drug cartels or street gangs, but by the billionaire President of the United States and his Ketamine-using, world's-richest-man enforcer.

This book is titled *American Carnage*. It could just as well have been titled American Tragedy. For what unfolded in the first months of 2025 is a tragedy of historic proportions, one that will forever change, and ultimately diminish, the United States, both in how it views itself and in how the rest of the world perceives it. America once confidently positioned itself as a shining city on a hill, as the country for whom no challenge was too great; the shattering events of 2025 dulled the shine and corroded the hill, leaving a denuded, morally impoverished landscape in their wake.

PART ONE

GROUND ZERO

Two days after the inauguration, Taly Lind was informed that her job at USAID was not in alignment with the new administration's priorities.

After more than a dozen years in foreign service, Lind had been hired to work on human rights and governance issues during Joe Biden's presidency, and her new title included the phrase "diversity, equity, inclusion and accessibility." For Trump, who had gone to war against DEI around the country during his election campaign — and who was now planning a raft of executive orders to essentially render illegal any reference to DEI, or DEI-related activity in any government agency or in any institution or organization seeking grants from the federal government — such programs were like a red flag waved at an angry bull. Taly Lind was immediately placed on Administrative Leave, told to go back to her house that she and her husband, a senior Foreign Service official, had been renting since he was assigned a posting in Hawaii, and to cease all work activities.

During Trump 1.0, Lind had been pleasantly surprised that, despite Trump's heated rhetoric on foreign aid, in reality many of the programs had continued apace — and the leadership that Trump had appointed to run USAID had maintained investments in sustainable development programs, in democracy-promoting activities, and in vital healthcare initiatives around the world. "The first Trump Administration had a USAID approach that made sense regarding foreign policy and how America wanted to show up in the world," she noted. But then came Trump 2.0, and it was an entirely different beast. Now, not only was the rhetoric over-the-top, but the Administration had come in fully armed and ready to wage war against agencies they saw no point in and wanted, for ideological reasons, to demolish. "We were," she recalled, "utterly sideswiped."

Lind and her colleagues had spent months girding for the possibility that Trump would attack DEI programs; they thought it was silly, but at the end of the day they were ready, if need be, to rewrite their manuals and work descriptions to eliminate any references to DEI. What they weren't ready for was the all-out assault launched against their organization and against them as individuals. "They just decapitated us," the 53-year-old said sadly, sitting in her home months later and pondering the unfathomable fact that the government had deliberately destroyed both her career and the agency whose work she had made a life mission. "For no reason and no benefit to anyone except Elon Musk."

The house that Lind retreated to was spacious, a five-bedroom atop a hill on the Hawaiian island of Oahu, overlooking the swanky Waikiki neighborhood of Honolulu, and was well outside of her and her husband's price range. But, after years in which he had been posted as a foreign service officer in Mumbai, India, and months in which she had been working with victims of devastating floods in Pakistan, by the summer of 2022 both of them were exhausted and ready to splurge. And so, they dipped into their savings and rented the house, which the owners had just built, while they waited for one or other, or both of them, to be sent overseas again. Now, however, their Xanadu became her purgatory, the place she waited while the government plotted to terminate her position and eliminate her pay. Once she was officially fired, she had calculated, her pension would top out at $23,000 a year — and she wouldn't be able to access it until she was 62. If she lived into her eighties, this represented a lifetime loss of millions of dollars compared to what she would have been able to retire on had she kept her job just a little longer.

When you get hired into the foreign service, you typically enter in at a level six, five, or four. Over time, you work your way up, eventually hitting a level one. Beyond level one, there are four more categories for the Senior Foreign Service employees. Once you get into these higher ranks and have at least twenty years of foreign service employment, you can retire at any point after the age of 50, Lind explained. The pension you receive is calculated by averaging the three highest annual salaries you were paid. For each of the first twenty years of service, you are eligible for 1.7 percent of that average top salary, and for each additional year, you get another one percent. You also are eligible for what is known as a Social Security supplement, to compensate for the fact that, at least until a recent reform, federal retirees weren't eligible for Social Security. And you get a lifetime of health insurance. It sounds complicated, but it's really quite simple; add it all up and you get an inflation-indexed pension that comes out to an amount heading toward two-thirds of your final salary, along with comprehensive healthcare coverage. In other words, it's enough to retire comfortably after a lifetime of public service.

But here's the rub. If you are fired as part of a broad reduction in force, and you haven't yet reached level one on the Foreign Service ranking system, your retirement is shredded. First off, you only get one percent of your salary for every year worked, instead of 1.7 percent. Then, instead of being able to access it in your fifties, you can't claim it until you're 62. You get no health benefits, and your pension is no longer inflation indexed.

Lind had been anticipating a comfortable retirement. Now, because of Elon Musk's determination to feed her job and her agency into the woodchipper, she was eligible for only a $23,000 a year pension and wouldn't even get that for another nine years. "So, I have lost millions of dollars if I live to be 85, if you add up what I would have got versus what I'm getting," Lind said, sobbing. "I was counting on this. All of this for nothing, for no reason. The American people are not benefitting from this in any way."

* * *

As a young woman, Lind had left her home in New York to study in Israel, the country where she had been born and in which she had lived the first few years of her life before her family had migrated to America. While there, she met the man she would later marry. It was all something of a whirlwind. When they tied the knot, she was only twenty, and he was all of twenty-two. They finished their studies, and she went on to work with youth groups trying to advance the peace process in the Middle East, while her husband joined the foreign service. For both of them, working overseas, and seeking ways to advance peace, became life-passions. They lived in countries around the Middle East and Asia. While he rose up the State Department career ladder, she worked with refugees, with people who had been trafficked by criminal syndicates, and with women at risk of being forced into prostitution. In 2009, she got hired by USAID.

Over time, Lind and her husband came to an agreement. While he was at the state department, his career would dictate where they lived; after he retired, she would work for another ten years and they would travel wherever her work took them. And, finally, she, too, would retire, on a senior-level foreign service pension, and they would have the money, in old age, to globe-trot the world together.

That, at least, was the plan. And then, even before it became clear just how broad was the attack on government agencies, and just how all-encompassing was the antipathy to the public sector, the incoming Trump administration made it clear they wanted to destroy USAID.

The agency was the most visible manifestation of American soft power around the globe. Its employees and contractors distributed medications for treating HIV/AIDS to millions of people, including pregnant women at risk of passing the disease to their babies, mainly in sub-Saharan Africa. It operated clinics to treat tuberculosis, hepatitis, malaria, Mpox, cholera, diarrhea, not to mention emergent diseases with pandemic potential such as Ebola. It vaccinated millions of children annually against polio. It ran medical trials around the world, testing new vaccines and other medicines and medical devices. When regions were at particular risk of famine, USAID personnel were there distributing to kids on the verge of death from starvation high-protein drinks and food bars, made up of a peanut paste-based product named Plumpy'Nut, that had been proven to bring starvation victims back from the brink. After major natural disasters in regions with no disaster-response infrastructure, USAID would be involved in the recovery efforts.

For decades, since it had been established during the first year of John Kennedy's presidency, these sorts of activities had won plaudits from across the political spectrum. USAID was broadly understood to be one of the crown jewels of American foreign policy, embraced by Republican and Democratic administrations alike as a relatively cheap way to project American power and win friends in countries around the world. Its supporters ran the gamut from Bernie Sanders to Mitch McConnell.

Somehow, however, in recent years USAID had become a bugbear for the various hard-right movements, and their conservative media eco-system, whose new brand of take-no-prisoners politics had coalesced around Trump's MAGA movement. Polls showed a majority of Americans were wildly misinformed about the costs of foreign aid, with many believing that the country spent as much as a quarter of its federal budget on such programs. In reality, the total spent on foreign aid was orders of magnitude less. The year before Trump was elected, the government spent just under $72 billion, roughly 1.2 percent of the federal budget, on foreign aid. Of that, somewhere in the region of half was sent USAID's way. It was little more than a blip on the federal spending radar; yet, for the fast-charging disrupters of Trump 2.0, it represented an unforgivable weakness — the distribution of resources to desperately poor people who couldn't generate a profit, or a monetizable rate of return, for America. That meant, in their worldview, it was simply throwing money down the toilet. On Truth Social eighteen days into his presidency, Trump posted that USAID's spending was "TOTALLY UNEXPLAINABLE... CLOSE IT DOWN!" Elon Musk, who would tweet during the first months of the new Administration about how too much empathy for others could lead to civilizational death, accused the agency of money-laundering and lambasted its employees for being "an arm of the radical-left globalists." Conspiracist broadcaster Alex Jones posted on X that USAID was responsible for a "mass theft of public funds."

Lind was the epitome of what a skilled foreign service public official should be. She spoke multiple languages; had worked in Morocco, Egypt, and Pakistan in the sixteen years that she had been with USAID, finishing up in Pakistan in 2022, the year that historic floods swamped much of the country for weeks on end; and, more recently, from her office in DC, had managed democracy and civil society programs in dozens of countries. She had seen the extraordinary bridge-building powers of the programs that USAID ran and understood the importance — far beyond their monetary value — of the relationships these programs nurtured. None of this protected her from the wrath of the new administration.

In the early days of the purges, roughly 2,000 USAID workers were told they would be fired; a staggering 60,000 contract workers overseas, the men and women who actually distributed medicines and injected vaccines and did all the other vital work, also lost their jobs and their income.

Experts at USAID had calculated the number of lives that would likely be lost over the following years as a result of the agency's cessation of operations. The figures were heartbreaking: an additional 18 million people would probably contract malaria over the coming decade, and 166,000 would die; millions of children would contract polio and 200,000 would be paralyzed; 1 million children would go untreated for severe malnutrition, and a significant proportion of these would die; tens of thousands more people would contract deadly hemorrhagic fevers such as Ebola. In addition, the world would see a thirty percent increase in the number of cases of drug-resistant tuberculosis, and millions more people would progress from having HIV to full-blown AIDS. When Boston University professor Brooke Nichols, an infectious disease mathematical modeler and health economist began tracking the impact of the cut-off of USAID work, she found extraordinary, and immediate, impacts: As a result of lack of access to medicines and treatments, 119,000 children and 57,000 adults had, she estimated, already died in the three months following USAID's destruction.

For Lind and others who had devoted their lives to public health overseas, words could barely begin to describe the sense of horror they felt. "I mean, they have blood on their hands," Lind said, crying bitter tears as she tried to wrap her head around the cascading calamity.

Now, as Taly Lind sat at home, essentially ordered by the government to twiddle her thumbs in exchange for her paycheck, the assault on USAID intensified. Each day brought new bad news: DOGE had entered their building, programs across the world were being cancelled, contractors weren't being paid for work already done, and life-saving medicines were being left in warehouses both Stateside and overseas because the staff on the ground had been ordered not to distribute them. So, too, food in famine zones had been left to rot for similar reasons and stockpiles of Plumpy'Nut servings, each package of which costs just a few cents to make and distribute, were stranded in warehouses in Rhode Island and elsewhere.

When a child was diagnosed as being close to death from starvation, the standard treatment involved three bags of Plumpy'Nut per day for six to eight weeks. Since each bag cost thirty cents to make, the total cost of saving that boy's or girl's life ran to somewhere between forty and fifty dollars. Given that Elon Musk had, in the latter months of 2024 and early 2025, as his wealth expanded by hundreds of billions of dollars, been making an average of $600 million *per day*, that meant that a single day of Musk's earnings could have provided an eight-week course of Plumpy'Nut to twelve million children. In Trump and Musk's extraordinary calculus, however, providing such life-saving interventions was now considered an unacceptable expense that was no longer in America's national interest.

Lind fumed. "The infrastructure of development has been severely damaged," she said. "All of these organizations, because they stopped paying them on a dime and didn't even pay for the work already done, from one day to the next were bankrupt. Under contract law, how is this legal? And apparently Congress doesn't give a shit. They sat back; it's mind-boggling to me. They have laid down and died. And I don't understand it."

Weeks after Lind had been told she could no longer work, with the USAID offices permanently closed, the overwhelming majority of its programs overseas shuttered, and the tattered remnants of the once-great agency being absorbed into Marco Rubio's State Department, the formal letters announcing a "Reduction In Force" were mailed out. The first batch of letters was sent to employees in late February, announcing that they would be terminated on April 24. These missives were riddled with errors, with many workers finding that they listed incorrect dates for when they had started working with the federal government and what rank they had reached in the civil service pay scale — all of which impacted what benefits they would be paid, how much severance money they would get, and the size of their retirement package. The letters seemed to have been written in a rush, by people who couldn't even be bothered to check the personnel files.

Then, in early March, the entire staff received notice, not from USAID's human resources department, which itself had been gutted, but from the Office of Personnel Management (the main personnel agency for the entire US government) that they would be fired either on July 1 or September 2. In the intervening months between the letters having been received and the date of the employees' termination, the workers were, like Lind, all expected to sit on their hands. She struggled to understand the economic rationale behind this. If it was genuinely about saving federal dollars, none of this added up. "We're getting paid to be on Administrative Leave," she marveled. "As a taxpayer, it makes me nauseous."

At 2:33 p.m. Mountain Time, on February 27, 2025, Natasha Miles's world also fell apart.

For five days, the 53-year-old atmospheric scientist, whose specialty involved taking, and interpreting, intricate measurements for urban carbon dioxide and methane emissions, had been driving west. She had worked at Penn State University for decades, since graduating from there with a PhD in atmospheric science, and for the past twenty years had been a research professor at its Institute of Energy and the Environment, on the main campus, at University Park. In recent years, she had received grant money from NOAA for her projects; she had also begun serving as a consultant to the agency. Eventually, her contacts at NOAA had suggested that she move over to work for the agency full-time and, after grappling with whether or not she wanted to leave academia, eventually she said "yes."

Miles was at the point in her life where she wanted to shake things up a little. Her two sons were grown — and both had enrolled to study at the university in which she worked. Her husband, a supercomputer expert, had moved to Illinois to take up a job at the state university campus in Urbana-Champaign. And she had become wary of the endless hustle for grant money to fund her research and her salary; far better, she reasoned, to take a federal job with stable pay and benefits at an agency that scientists the world over looked to for data on how and why the earth's climate was changing.

"The job was perfect for me, working with a group of people who are really great and dedicated to climate science," she explained. She would be part of the largest network in the world dedicated to measuring CO_2 and methane emissions, with colleagues who flew planes to take measurements, who climbed up high towers to place instruments, who ran global projects to capture air samples that could then be shipped back to NOAA's Boulder, Colorado, office for analysis. Cumulatively, this work allowed for extraordinarily accurate readings of changes in the atmospheric levels of greenhouse gasses from one year to the next.

And so, in August of 2024, the erstwhile professor began the process of migrating her work over from the university to NOAA.

The agency wanted her out in Boulder, on the eastern edge of the Rockies, in its sprawling cinderblock complex from which one could literally walk out the door and be at the base of the soaring, shard-like mountains, the reddish rocks heavy with iron. It wasn't a hard sell; over the years, Miles had been there numerous times to consult with NOAA experts; she loved the landscape, the laid-back western culture of Boulder, its hip cafes and restaurants, its beautiful art galleries. Deep into middle age, she had, during the pandemic, taken up skiing, and relished the prospect of packing up her green Volkl skis and boots and, on her days off work, heading up to the Eldora ski resort outside of Boulder. She was excited, too, to take her twelve-year-old dog, Mia, a lively red heeler-brittany mix, on walks along Boulder Creek and up into the canyons and mountains beyond.

Miles arranged to rent a small Airbnb studio attached to a capacious wooden chalet in the mountains six miles out of town. It was a challenge to drive to from Boulder, up a series of switchbacks that went from paved to gravel to red clay as it got further out of town, and she worried that even with the snow tires her car was now equipped with, she would get snowed in when the storms blew through the mountains; but she craved the fresh air and the solitude, she wanted to surround herself with the sounds of nature. She would, she hoped, stay in the Airbnb for a couple of months, as she oriented herself, and then look for more permanent housing.

By the time all the paperwork had been completed, election season had come and gone, and with it had arrived a second Trump presidency. There was a lot of noise about Project 2025, a constant barrage of rumors about huge cuts coming to government. Trump had made no secret of his distaste for all things environmental, especially those relating to climate change. He was promising to appoint anti-environmental ideologues into key government positions, and he had expressed a desire to roll back the major environmental initiatives undertaken by the Biden administration. But, Trump had made much the same noise after he had moved into the White House in 2017, with his MAGA paraphernalia and his gold baubles, and by and large government agencies like NOAA had been able to continue doing what they had been doing for years — conducting their research, building up their databases of information, helping the broader public prepare for weather emergencies, assisting scientists around the country with their projects. And so, this time around, despite the more programmatic nature of a Trump administration fortified by the ultra-conservative theorists of Project 2025, Miles initially wasn't too worried. After the paperwork was finalized on January 25, she began working as a hybrid employee, flying to Denver and driving north to NOAA for a few days of in-person work, then back east to Pennsylvania, where she was still packing up her house and her life, to work remotely.

As the swirl of DOGE activity in DC intensified, she calculated what was absolutely essential to have with her in her little studio out west, and dumped those must-have items — clothes, ski gear, Prince tennis racket, backpack, sleeping bag, a few household items and books and mementoes — into her dark blue Hyundai Tucson hybrid SUV, kitted out with a travel cage for Mia. On February 22, she looked around her home, which she had decided to keep ownership of for now, one last time, walked out to her vehicle, and set off on a 2,000 mile road trip west.

It was going to be an adventure; of that she had no doubt. Miles and Mia stopped off first in Indiana for a couple of days, to stay with Miles' parents and to visit her sister's family. They went from there to Champaign, so that Miles could see her husband. They stayed a night somewhere in Kansas — just a place to rest after a long day of driving, she couldn't subsequently remember exactly where — and then, on day five, set out for Boulder.

* * *

An hour outside of Boulder, Natasha Miles's phone began to ring. It was 2:33 p.m. Her boss was on the other end of the line.

"Have you checked your email?" she asked. Miles hadn't; she'd been driving. "You need to."

The scientist found an exit ramp from the highway, pulled her SUV off to the side of the road, and opened up her email on her phone. There it was, in black and white: Miles' job no longer met the needs of the new administration and was being eliminated. As of 5 p.m. that day, she would no longer be a federal employee. She sat there, in her car, Mia whining in the cage behind her, flabbergasted, crying. "You're supposed to be saving for retirement at this point and not be unemployed," she thought to herself. And then she thought *who on earth is going to do this vital work now?* "If we're not making these measurements," she explained weeks later, after she had had time to process what had happened, "you can't improve on mitigation. You can't improve on mitigation if you don't know what's happening."

What could she do but continue driving west? Miles took some deep breaths, tried to calm the rising panic, and continued onto Boulder, up the canyons, along the dirt roads, and to her little studio. She realized she had just landed two thousand miles from home, with no income coming in, that she had no information about whether or not she still had health insurance — and thus no information on whether she would be able to fill prescriptions for the medications she needed to keep her Crohn's Disease under control and thus herself out of the hospital — and nobody she could call or email at work (her work email was de-activated by the government at 5 p.m. that day) who knew what was going on and could help her navigate this process.

One minute, she was a revered scientist, the next minute, as something approaching an American Cultural Revolution picked up steam, she had been placed on the new administration's trash heap. A week earlier, a manic Elon Musk had turned up at the Conservative Political Action Conference convention quite literally brandishing a chainsaw on stage, whooping it up to the delighted crowd as he described demolishing entire government agencies at speed. It was a grotesque, gaudy spectacle and one that left America's allies around the world entirely bemused. This wasn't, to put it mildly, what one expected from the world's pre-eminent democracy. Now, Miles realized, she herself had ended up on the wrong end of that chainsaw.

On the other side of the country, Kelsey Hendrix was also facing the loss of her job at NOAA.

Growing up in a conservative, Evangelical family in the little town of Moresville, North Carolina, in the 1990s and early 2000s, Kelsey Hendrix had always wanted to be a scientist. But life, she found, had a way of playing tricks on people.

At school, she discovered that despite her love of STEM classes, she actually wasn't very good at hard, cold science. None of it came naturally to her. No matter how much she fantasized about working in labs or hunting for new energy sources or playing around with combinations of molecules to create new materials, the reality was that she struggled.

Instead, she found herself thriving in her psychology classes and in the social sciences.

Hendrix knew that she had to make the most of what she had. Through a genetic misfiring, she had been born largely blind — "I kinda wish it was an accident," she would tell people, laughing with her own private sense of dark humor as she recounted the drama that had accompanied her since the day she was born. "That would have been a funnier story." She suffered from severe rheumatoid arthritis. And she had been diagnosed with attention deficit disorder.

There were, Hendrix seemed to believe, two ways she could go given the hurdles life had thrown her way: she could curl up in a ball and be depressed, or she could make the most of what she had. Hendrix, who runs optimistic, chose to make the most of what she had. If the fates didn't want her to be a scientist, well, dammit, she would study something else. In the early 2010s, she was admitted to the University of North Carolina, Charlotte — close to home, but not too close, and, the biggest draw, the campus at which her boyfriend was enrolled — and started studying for a double major in psychology and criminal justice. In her senior year, she was accepted for an internship with the army's JAG office. A year later, she hit the job market, armed with her two bachelors' degrees from a top-tier public university. She didn't know exactly what she wanted to do, but she figured life would find a way to tell her.

* * *

At first, Hendrix hit a wall. She had a good degree, and had spent a year working with JAG, but now, as the decade began to wind down, she was applying for jobs and somehow never ending up with an offer. The young UNC graduate began to suspect that her blindness was scaring potential employers off.

Then, in 2019, the fates intervened again. She was on her way to yet another job interview when her stomach began to be wracked by pain. It was clear she wouldn't be able to sit through the interview, so Hendrix turned around, went back to her apartment, collapsed onto her bed, and turned on her laptop and its visual assistance programs. As the pain subsided, she clicked onto a virtual career fair and started navigating around the site, popping in at one virtual stall after the next, chatting with the people at the tables hawking their companies and organizations, presenting their job opportunities. Finally, at a table for the US Department of Commerce, a contractor asked her for her résumé, skimmed over it and requested that she come up to DC for more discussions.

A few months later, Hendrix found herself with her dream job. She wasn't a scientist, true, but she would be working with scientists. Hendrix had been hired on as a contractor by the National Oceanic and Atmospheric Administration, one of the government's premier scientific agencies, putting together the paperwork for consultants and contractors to work on specific projects around weather modelling, climate change, rain and snow and drought predictions, and the myriad other areas of expertise that had turned NOAA into one of the world's go-to places for data on how the earth's oceans and atmosphere functioned.

"In June, I moved to DC and it was awesome," she recalled, her voice limned with enthusiasm and the raw excitement that comes with being young and leaning into new experiences. "I fell in love with the city and it was awesome. I loved NOAA and I loved the people I worked with."

Three years and a pandemic later, NOAA moved her position from that of being a contractor to being an actual employee, meaning she would have a government salary and benefits. On an hourly basis, it represented a pay-cut from her work as a contractor, but it offered security and a chance for promotion. Hendrix leapt at the chance. On the civil service pay-scale, she was now a "GS9," with a starting salary of $64,000.

And then came the purge.

* * *

In the weeks after Donald Trump's second inauguration, Hendrix and her colleagues desperately tried to stay atop of all the rumors. They knew that Trump was promising to slash the number of government employees. They, like everyone else, had seen Elon Musk's elevation to cutter-in-chief, making the world's richest man arguably the most influential figure in DC.

Hendrix's crew were all too aware that Musk's new organization, with a scary-sounding acronym — DOGE — was on the prowl, looking for agencies to obliterate and employees to fire. They had, by mid-February, received their "Fork In The Road" emails, urging them to accept a "deferred resignation" offer that would pay them for months to stay home from the office while they looked for "more productive" work in the private sector. "We knew people in other agencies were getting cut. We knew we would probably get cut," Hendrix recalled. But, because her department was the one that was writing the contracts that held the entire web of employees and consultants and contractors together, she and her colleagues were fairly confident that they would escape the axe; after all, even a slimmed-down agency presumably needs the people who make possible the hiring and firing of other workers, and the whole consultant-and-contractor ecosystem upon which so much of the federal system rests.

Of course, in hindsight she realized that the cuts weren't being made strategically. The young DOGE engineers, with absurd monikers such as Big Balls, who had been given such extraordinary powers over the lives of millions of federal employees, over the functioning of the federal government, and over the well-being of all the tens of millions of Americans who, on a daily basis, rely on government services, weren't thinking about how to maintain the functionality of agencies like NOAA. Rather they were looking for the low-hanging fruit, the probationary employees who could easily be terminated without going through lengthy processes. And, because Hendrix had only recently moved over from being a consultant to being an employee, she was easy to pluck off of the government tree.

"No one is safe really," she concluded, after the fact. On February 27, her office began being hit by the mass firings. "It was me and another probationary employee on my team." Both of them opened their emails to find a letter telling them that their "ability, knowledge, and skills do not fit your agency's current needs," that they were being fired for "poor performance" — despite the fact that Hendrix was a new enough employee that she hadn't yet had a performance review. The email arrived in her inbox at 3:42 p.m. The time of her termination was listed as 5 p.m.

In a daze, Hendrix had to hand in her government computer, was locked out of her email, and, apart from the six days of annual leave that she had accumulated and which was paid out to her, was given no severance pay. Her health insurance was good for a month but would then be cut off — when it was, she would have to stop taking the biologic, the cost of which could run to a staggering $9,000 per month, that kept her severe arthritis at bay, and would have to fall back on the entirely inadequate stopgap measures of over-the-counter ibuprofen and cheap prescription steroids. Meanwhile, her dental and vision insurance would end as soon as did her last pay period. With black humor, she noted that since she was blind she wouldn't have been using the vision insurance anyway; but that the lack of dental coverage worried her — she hoped she didn't fall down and knock out a tooth.

In the weeks that followed, none of the paperwork that she needed in order to enroll in the government equivalent of COBRA, which would have let her buy into that health insurance for the next several months, was sent her way. No information was provided employees on how to access health insurance through the Obamacare public marketplaces — Hendrix was left to google basic information on this. Nor was the worker separation paperwork mailed to her that she required in order to be able to file for unemployment. She thought about applying for Medicaid, so that she could access her arthritis drugs, but then she realized that to qualify for that she would have to drain her life savings so as to appear more genuinely impoverished; and that, to her, seemed a Faustian bargain.

Around the huge federal bureaucracy, as the cuts kicked in similar stories could be heard; in their rush to slash the government pay-roll, DOGE and their department-level enforcers were working so fast that they weren't sending the most basic severance paperwork, leaving the fired employees stranded, with no access to healthcare and, since they had no real proof beyond a series of emails that they were no longer federal employees, no ability to receive unemployment insurance.

Those weren't the only corners they were cutting; as Musk and Trump pushed to centralize vast tranches of government data to a previously unimaginable degree, they began violating a host of privacy regulations, bulldozing their way into data bases at everything from the IRS and the Department of Health and Human Services to the Department of Housing and Urban Development and the State Department in an effort to find, and deport, undocumented immigrants, and to root out purported fraud in safety net programs.

Weeks after she had been fired, Hendrix was struggling to maintain the optimism that had carried her so far in life. "I don't want to be unemployed again for a long time. I don't want to lose our apartment," she said. She and her boyfriend were staying afloat — though they had cancelled a long-planned vacation — but she worried that since he was a contractor for another government agency his income could also suddenly vanish as Musk's teams of operatives continued to cut swathes through federal agencies. "It's been an interesting time," she said, dryly. "I kind of expected it; it still stung. We have a chat going with all the people terminated at NOAA. Reactions range from mine — I kinda expected it — to people being just devastated."

In her bleaker moments, when she wasn't being distracted by her pets or visiting with her friends, when she wasn't walking through the spring cherry blossoms in DC and touching the trees to feel the gentle blooms, Hendrix thought she might never again find a job to truly match her skill set. She had resigned herself to the likelihood of downward mobility. "I have to pay bills. We have to survive somehow and not die. If I have to work in a call center, then that's what I have to do. The job market is saturated. It was hard before they fired tens of thousands of us. 275,000 federal employees and contractors have been fired in March alone. We are competing against the influx of new people who have lost their jobs."

What made it an even more bitter pill to swallow was the fact that so many people around the country simply didn't understand the vital nature of the work that agencies such as NOAA did — work that helped farmers navigate changing weather patterns, that helped pilots avoid flying into storms, that helped cities prepare for hurricanes and tornados. On social media platforms, it wasn't uncommon to see gloating, vengeful posts about how federal employees were finally getting their comeuppance. "People think we're just office bureaucrats making ridiculous amounts of money, sitting in our DC offices and playing Tetrus all day. But that is not the case. We had jobs, doing important work — work that now isn't going to get done."

In the past, that hatred of government hadn't been the case. In Gwinnett County, Georgia, about a forty minute drive outside of Atlanta, it didn't matter whether you were a Republican, a Democrat, or an independent, you knew people who worked for the Centers for Disease Control; and, likely as not, until the recent hyper-politicization of views on the public sector, you felt an abiding sense of pride in knowing that the world's preeminent public health organization was an anchor to the surrounding community.

That was certainly the case for Aryn Backus when she was growing up, the third of four siblings and half-siblings, in the late 1990s and 2000s in the fast-growing suburb of Snellville. The parents of several of her friends were CDC employees, and everything about the organization seemed cool to her; its staff were working to prevent disease outbreaks and to understand how illnesses spread, and all of them radiated a powerful sense of public service.

Backus's family was solidly middle-class, and her upbringing reflected that. For years, she did ballet. She played clarinet in her middle-school marching band and was in the color guard dance line for the marching band in her high school. She was a cross-country runner and an avid reader.

In sophomore year of high school, she became friends with a boy on the drum line. Three years later, they would start dating.

They would both attend the University of Georgia's Athens campus, where she would study for a degree in communications — and down the road, after she had completed a master's degree in public health at Emory University, they would end up marrying.

All the while, Backus was thinking about how to get a communications job at the CDC. When she was at Emory, one of the country's top schools for public health, she was taught by professors who either had worked for, or still had gigs with, the organization. For her work study, she did a CDC internship at the organization's Chamblee Campus, with the Office of Safety, Security and Asset Management, learning the ropes for how to do internal communications in the event of an emergency. The internship straddled the end of the Obama presidency and the start of Trump's first presidency — and, because of that, ended up being truncated when the new president announced a federal hiring freeze, meaning that she couldn't be reappointed to finish her work study. It didn't dampen her enthusiasm for the CDC.

Backus graduated from her master's program in 2018. She was $75,000 in debt — a stunning amount that, at six percent interest, meant that without any relief she would be paying upwards of one thousand dollars a month for the next ten years. But she hoped that if she could get a job in the public sector, she would ultimately qualify for a loan forgiveness program. If she didn't, she wasn't sure exactly how she would cope; after all, in the Atlanta region she would likely start out at the CDC with a salary in the mid-fifties. Factor in the cost of housing, utilities, and all the other expenses that made up daily life, and that one thousand dollars seemed like a mountain to climb each month.

Seemingly on cue, an Emory alumna who was now working at the CDC reached out to her as she was getting ready to graduate and asked if she was interested in becoming a fellow with the ORISE program, aimed at bringing young public health workers who had recently received their masters' or PhDs into the CDC. Backus could hardly hide her delight; it was a perfect opportunity and she could start a month after graduating; if it panned out, it would set her on a path for student debt relief.

And that was how it began. She did two years with ORISE. Then, during the Covid crisis she was tapped to work on communicating with the public about the pandemic. And after that, in early 2022, she took a contracting job at the Office of Smoking and Health. In November 2024, just after the election, she was offered a job doing basically the same work but as a full-time employee. After six and a half years with the CDC, bouncing from one office to the next, it appeared as if she was now in a secure position. Her pay had increased, she was getting benefits, and she was doing important work educating the public on the dangers of smoking and on ways to make it easier to quit the habit.

* * *

It didn't take long after Trump was inaugurated, on January 20, for Backus to realize she might have to dramatically recalibrate her expectations. Emails started hitting her in-box, seemingly from random people outside of the government email system, urging her to leave her "low-productivity" job and seek work in the private sector. Other emails circulated that told her and her colleagues that anyone caught trying to do DEI-related work under the radar would immediately be terminated. Still other missives insisted the CDC communications teams delete all reference to transgender and non-binary people in their press releases and other files. She found out that her supervisor had been asked to provide a list to the Office of Personnel Management of all probationary employees, and to then indicate whether or not they were mission-critical workers.

In early February, mass firings started hitting different government departments and agencies. As the month progressed, the firings intensified. DOGE squads were basically targeting one department after the next, gaining access to their employee and pay data, to their contracts with contractors and with grantees, and then orchestrating a mass culling of newer hires.

All of which made for a nerve-racking Valentines Day. All that day, as Backus desperately tried to focus on the upcoming launch of a "tips from former smokers campaign," the rumors intensified; DOGE had arrived at the CDC with its metaphorical chainsaws. The National Center for Injury Prevention and Control was being hit; the National Center for Chronic Disease Prevention and Health Promotion was being decimated.

When she made it to 5 p.m. without having been fired, Backus breathed a sigh of relief. Perhaps, after all, she would be safe. She went home, too worn out to celebrate Valentine's Day. When, hours later, the CDC director sent out an email to staff informing them that terminations had taken place, Backus again thought she had dodged a bullet — after all, she still hadn't received any word that she was being fired. The next evening, a Saturday, she relaxed enough to drop off her one year old son with her mother, and go on a belated Valentine's date with her husband. They drove into the swanky uptown Atlanta neighborhood of Buckhead, ate dinner, accompanied by a bottle of white wine, at an Italian restaurant — they shared a charcuterie dish, and, for her main, she ordered a lobster risotto — and then headed over to a dessert place for cheesecake and a flourless torte. By the time they had swung by her parents to pick up their child and then driven home it was eleven o'clock.

The next morning, Aryn got up early to feed her son. As she was doing this, her phone buzzed, alerting her to a text from a friend at the CDC. *Had she checked her work email recently?* No, she texted back. *You need to do so*, her friend replied, and then told her that she [the friend] had just been terminated. "I said, in my brain, 'well, shit!'" Aryn Backus recalled. She finished feeding her baby, logged onto her work email, and, sure enough, there was an email, from 7:35 p.m. the previous evening. It wasn't from a person, but was from a new email address, Employeenotification@CDC.gov, that had, in recent weeks, been sending out mass emails, usually about unpleasant topics seemingly designed to make employees' lives miserable; she and her colleagues assumed it had been set up by the DOGE crew. The subject line was a combination of ominous and phishing-like. "Read this immediately," It was the sort of tagline that smelled of a scam. The text within the email itself was hardly more reassuring. "Good afternoon. Please read the two attachments to this email immediately. Thank you for your service to the American public." If she didn't know it was a real email, with real consequences for her, she might well have deleted it and not opened up the attachments. After all, the most basic cyber-security training tells you to be suspicious of an email like that. Instead, with trepidation, she downloaded the documents. The first informed her that she was "not fit for continued employment, because your ability, knowledge and skills do not fit Agency needs; and your performance has not been adequate to justify your further employment at the Agency." The second informed her that she could appeal the first.

Backus was stunned. She knew that she was a stellar worker — that was why the CDC had hired her months earlier instead of leaving her as a contractor. She also knew that being fired for poor performance would both make it harder to qualify for unemployment benefits and also make it next-to-impossible to ever get a federal job again. And she also knew that whoever had authored the letter, or whichever AI program had spewed it out, wasn't even making the slightest effort to be accurate. She would find out, within days, that all 800 of the probationary employees who had been fired at the CDC had received the exact same letter; in the rush to ditch them, all had been arbitrarily given a black mark against their name that could easily hobble them for the rest of their careers.

Adrian M (she asked for her last name not to be used) had also gotten a letter, this one from the Centers for Disease Control, informing her that she was being fired from the CDC because her performance wasn't up to par. It infuriated her.

An African American woman who had grown up in rural Tennessee, Adrian knew more than a little about prejudice. She knew that to get ahead in life a Black woman frequently had to work twice as hard as other people, simply to overcome all of the prejudice that came their way. She knew all the stereotypes — that Black women were angry, emotional, quick to fly off the handle. And she knew that, too often, they were seen as charity cases — as people who had only gotten their education and their jobs because of affirmative action or, more recently, DEI.

In Adrian's experience, the reverse held. She recalled all the times that teachers in her schools had assumed the worst of her, simply because of the color of her skin; had avoided calling her to answer questions; had made it clear they didn't think she was going anywhere in life. She recalled the group of white teenage boys, in high school, who fashioned themselves as a clique self-titled The Rednecks, whose leader made a point of body slamming her as he walked down the hallway. She recalled the instances when fellow students had lobbed the N-word at her.

Adrian's mother had worked long hours to make sure that her two daughters didn't go without. Adrian remembered her older sister and her being dropped off at their aunt's house early mornings, so that they could catch the school bus from there; her mother had to work long shifts at a local Levi Strauss factory. After school, the bus would return the girls to their grandparents' home — their mother would still be at work.

Growing out of her own experiences, their mother would always tell them they should learn to be independent, to be able to support themselves, to never have to rely on others to pay basic expenses. When she got a cell phone, she was expected to pay her own monthly bills; when she got a car, she was responsible for the insurance. Adrian took the life-lesson to heart. After school, she enrolled in classes at the Northeast State Technical Community College, and then, after a couple years, transferred over to Eastern Tennessee State University (ETSU), where she quickly worked out that she was both good at, and enjoyed, public health classes, "teaching people to protect themselves and to protect their health." To pay her way, she worked multiple minimum wage jobs — as a staffer at a kindercare center; on the late night shift at a local Wendy's; and, finally, as a personal care provider for an old lady suffering from dementia, whose family were willing to pay helpers in order to be able to keep her in her home. She topped up the earnings from these jobs by taking out student loans. Some years, she had to work so many hours that she would end up dropping out for a semester. Other years, she would have to retake classes because she didn't have the bandwidth to focus as she needed to on her studies.

In 2009, just before Adrian's twenty-fifth birthday, her mother died of a stroke, while vacationing in Virginia, at the age of only 49. A long-time smoker, she had been suffering from massively elevated blood pressure — and had stopped taking the medications that her doctors had prescribed because they made her feel too ill; later, it would come to light that the particular medication she was on frequently triggered adverse reactions in African American patients, a phenomenon not discovered in the clinical trials because they weren't designed to look at differing reactions from patients of different racial and ethnic backgrounds.

Knocked sideways by her mother's premature death, it took Adrian a decade to finally finish college. But, throughout, she knew that she eventually wanted to end up at the CDC. Her mother's death, and the failure to identify the medication side-effects experienced by many African Americans, had shocked her, and, as importantly, had made her realize the critical mission of an agency like the CDC, and its educational role in informing medical practitioners and the general public about risks to health caused both by behaviors such as smoking and also by taking medications that were likely to trigger bad reactions.

After several years — and several detours — Adrian finally was able to land a job at the CDC in Atlanta; she spent a couple years on a CDC-funded public health fellowship in Cedar Rapids, Iowa — a place where, she found out, the snows were so cold that ice sheets formed over the sidewalk; her responsibilities included working on chronic disease issues, health literacy campaigns, and environmental health work around air quality. She helped reduce local childhood asthma rates with a campaign to get school bus drivers and parents to turn off their vehicles while waiting for children outside of schools, rather than keeping the engines idling and spewing pollutants into the air. She was also involved in checking schools for the presence of radon. Evenings and weekends, she studied online for a master's degree in public health, taking classes offered by Capella University, out of Minnesota. Somehow, she also squeezed in additional paid work, as a receptionist at a local pediatric clinic. Add up the number of hours Adrian was working or studying and it seemed a miracle she ever had time to sleep.

When the fellowship ended, Adrian bounced between an array of contract jobs, doing work on dialysis and other illnesses for the CDC, then, in mid-2019, moving over to work for the Office of Smoking Health, and finally, a year into the Covid pandemic, taking on social media communications duties. Throughout these many years, she rented a basement apartment, scrimping on rent so as to save money to one day be able to afford to buy a house.

In September 2024, she finally got the call she had been waiting for, seemingly for her entire adult life: she was offered a full-time job at the CDC, like Aryn Backus in the Office of Smoking and Health. Now, finally, she had job security, and could put a downpayment down on her very own home. She found a three bedroom, two bathroom, on three quarters of an acre of land, and she and her two dogs — both Jack Russell mixes — moved in. "I was very happy, very proud." Her grandfather, whom she had always looked to for approval, phoned to tell her that he was also proud of her.

* * *

The same evening that Bachus was fired for poor performance, Adrian was also terminated. She, too, was informed that her performance wasn't up to par; and, for her, the subtext stung even more. She felt that people in the federal government who had spent months railing against DEI — Trump had grotesquely insinuated, days after his inauguration, that DEI hires in the military and the FAA were responsible for a fatal air crash over the Potomac River — simply assumed that she was a poor performer because of the color of her skin and her gender. "I'm being called a poor performer, and my knowledge and skills don't meet the needs of the agency," she said, incredulously. "My knowledge and skills *came* from the agency. I wouldn't have had my job if my skills weren't good."

The idea that she, as a Black woman from the South, had somehow had it easy in life because of her skin color made her laugh, it was so absurd. "We have to tow a specific line as Black women," she felt. "Because people are easily offended. We can be deemed aggressive. I'm always held to a higher standard. *I only got here because I'm an African American woman?* No, that's not possible; that's not how it happens." And the notion that the CDC could be forbidden from focusing research or educational outreach efforts on specific, under-represented, marginalized groups, be they racial minorities or sexual minorities, made her want to weep. She knew that, as a result of the decisions being made to corral what CDC communications and research could and couldn't cover, "people are going to die."

On a more personal level, she was terrified that everything she had managed to accomplish in her life was now at risk. Having poured her heart and soul into building her career and saving money for a home, she saw that everything was up in the air again. "Am I going to be able to keep my house?" she asked herself. "Am I going to find another job?"

And all for what? So far as Adrian could see, the Trump administration and the DOGE shock-troops were simply in it to burn everything down. "We have a system set up in America for a reason," she believed. "And when you start breaking down the system, you're breaking down America."

The officials at the Consumer Financial Protection Bureau felt that sentiment acutely. Daniel Dodd-Ramirez's road to the CFPB had been a winding one. Born in Brazil to a Colombian mother and a US father — the couple met while he was serving in the Peace Corps in the late 1960s — Daniel had spent his first few years in Brazil and then Colombia before the family moved to a sprawling, only partially finished homestead, on fourteen acres of land, in rural Maine, in 1977. After his parents separated, his mother got a job in a factory, and Daniel, his twin brother and his sister were left largely to their own devices as their mother worked long hours in a local factory to earn enough money to cover the basic bills.

The family were poor enough to qualify for food stamps. And the house was very much a work in progress — its outhouse that served as their bathroom bitterly cold in the harsh New England winters. Daniel struggled to focus in school, finishing up near the bottom of his high school graduation class. Afterwards, he picked up whatever work he could at local restaurants and bars.

In the early 1990s, Dodd-Ramirez's mother, whose financial situation had improved after she had remarried and sold the old house, offered to take Daniel and his siblings on a trip back to Colombia to visit family in Bogotá. *Why not?* Daniel thought. After all, he didn't have anything urgent keeping him tied to Maine. Once there, he and his brother decided to stay. It was, to say the least, an interesting time in Colombia. The decades-old civil war was still simmering, and Pablo Escobar's Medellín Cartel was in an increasingly bloody fight with the Colombian authorities. Not infrequently, bombs would go off in the capital. Scary, yes; but fascinating at the same time.

Daniel and his brother moved in with their grandmother and began teaching English. Over the next four years, things started to click into place for Daniel. He found the academic focus that he had lacked in school; the sense of drift that he had had in his teens and early twenties was replaced by life goals. He wanted to make social change. By the time he returned Stateside, in 1995, Daniel was ready to apply to college. He did so, taking an undergraduate degree in Hispanic Studies at the University of Southern Maine, and following it up with a master's degree from the School for International Training, in Brattleboro, Vermont. His thesis was on Intercultural Management. As a way to push back against the depressive tendencies he had begun experiencing, he also began meditating, ultimately going on a series of silent retreats that ranged up to 45 days in length. Not talking was, he found, the easy part; far harder was processing all of the images and emotions that flooded his mind during that silence.

Over the next decades, Dodd-Ramirez put together a career helping others. For several years, he worked as a community organizer in Miami. Then, shortly after he'd met, at a meditation retreat, the woman who would become his wife, he got offered a job with the city government in Savannah, Georgia. Daniel was tasked with starting up a nonprofit called Step Up Savannah, which was hoping to reduce the high poverty rate in many of the city's neighborhoods. Set up as a public-private partnership, it had 36 board members, drawn in equal parts from grassroots groups in poor parts of town, from the city's business and political leadership, as well as from social service agencies. And it had a mandate to get creative in tackling engrained social problems.

That's exactly what Dodd-Ramirez did. In a large room in the civic center, the organization set up what they called a "poverty simulator" — one that had been designed by low-income single mothers in Missouri. They created storylines for generic low-income residents that participants from the world of politics and business could role-play in order to familiarize themselves with the daily challenges faced by people in poverty; and gave them individualized packages to take them through the exercise — small amounts of cash; in some cases, if they were playing someone gang-involved, even a [toy] gun; and other accoutrements. Each session lasted one hour, with every fifteen minutes representing a week in the life of the person playing the role. Participants, many of whom were conservative by temperament, came into the exercise thinking all that poor people needed to do was pull themselves up by their bootstraps. They were confronted with all the indignities and inconveniences of poverty — from trying to find a check cashing outlet because they didn't have a bank account, to looking for public transport options in areas badly serviced by bus and train routes because they didn't have a car, through to having to work out what to do with their young children when they went on a job interview.

As the work picked up steam, and as growing numbers of people went through the simulator, so more business leaders had epiphanies about the complexity of poverty — and many of them proceeded to put their money where their mouth was, looking to get involved in an array of local anti-poverty efforts. Residents were given access to financial literacy classes, to job training programs, to apprentice programs and more. All told, upwards of ninety organizations joined a coalition to work on these anti-poverty efforts in the community. In consequence, Step Up Savannah — billed as an innovative anti-poverty effort in the conservative Deep South — garnered international attention. Journalists from the BBC, Al-Jazeera, and many other outlets journeyed to Georgia to see the program in action.

The success of Step Up Savannah increased Dodd-Ramirez's visibility in anti-poverty circles. He was getting something of a name for himself as someone willing to experiment in order to bend the arc a bit toward bettering the lives of low-income Americans. In 2014, he applied for a high-level position at the still fairly new Consumer Financial Protection Bureau, and shortly afterwards was given a job offer. He would be in charge of more than a dozen people, putting in place national strategies and community partnerships all aimed at helping low income consumers protect their financial assets and better their financial well-being. Other offices, following the mandates established in the CFPB's founding legislation, the Dodd-Frank Wall Street Reform and Consumer Protection Act, focused their attentions on protecting students, veterans, and older Americans. The bureau, originally the brainchild of Massachusetts senator Elizabeth Warren, employed economists, attorneys, researchers, and others who could put together deep dives into the dubious lending practices of companies they were investigating.

It all added up to a phenomenal deal for taxpayers: the American public got a raft of protections against predatory lenders, but didn't have to pay a dime — for the CFPB was funded by the Federal Reserve, out of a pool of funds raised by levying fees on banks. That didn't mean, however, that it was universally popular; many Republicans had opposed the agency since the day it began operations, in late July 2011, disliking its regulations and believing it needlessly hobbled financial institutions and put an unfair crimp in companies' profits. Trump had mused about trying to close it down during his first presidency, though ultimately decided against picking that fight, opting instead to appoint Mick Mulvaney — a conservative Congressman who had spent years railing against the Bureau — as acting director, in which capacity he set to work trimming some of its functions and reorienting its work toward encouraging low-income Americans to save more money, rather than going after bad actors in the world of finance. Two elections later, as Trump campaigned again for the White House in 2024, many of his advisors, especially those coming out of Project 2025, made clear that their hostility to the bureau and its mission had in no way dimmed.

All by way of saying that, for Dodd-Ramirez and his colleagues, it hardly came as a surprise that Trump 2.0 wasn't shaping up to be the best of times for the CFPB. What they didn't expect, though, was the sheer scale, and speed, of the DOGE assault unleashed against them.

At the start of February, Trump fired Biden's CFPB director, Rohit Chopra and replaced him with acting director Russell Vought — one of the architects of Project 2025 and Trump's choice to head up the Office of Management and Budget. Vought was an ideologue, stridently opposed to regulatory agencies that could, and did, place limits on the activities of private companies. Like anti-tax activist Grover Norquist decades earlier, Vought seemed to want to shrink government down so much that what was left of it could be strangled in a bathtub. Putting him in charge of the CFPB was a clear sign that Trump wanted to destroy the entire operation.

Days later, shadowy DOGE operatives started meeting at the CFPB, much as they were doing at other agencies, such as USAID, that they would then proceed to destroy. Vought's henchman, an economist named Mark Calabria who had been an advisor both to Vice President Mike Pence during Trump 1.0 and also to the libertarian-leaning Cato Institute, ordered its 1,500 staff to stop their work. Vought closed its headquarters, and he attempted to deprive it of all funding by writing to inform the Federal Reserve that it didn't need to draw on any additional funds to pay for its work going forward.

Rumors circulated that the CFPB was going to be the main sacrificial victim of an upcoming Valentine's Day massacre — that with one stroke of a pen the entire staff would be fired. In response, the National Treasury Employees Union, the union representing non-managerial workers at the bureau, went to court seeking a temporary restraining order to stop such a cull from being undertaken. Dodd-Ramirez had been slated to go on a long silent meditation retreat, but now he worried that if he did, he wouldn't be able to advocate for his team at a critical moment; so he pushed it off until July.

In the end, the massacre didn't quite pan out as the rumors had anticipated. Instead of being fired in February, the vast majority of workers at the CFPB ended up being put on Administrative Leave. Or at least that was how they understood it, based on the emails they had received that told them this. It wasn't how the Trump team liked to talk about it; when Trump's nominee to be permanent director of the CFPB, Jonathan McKernen, testified during his Senate confirmation hearings in late February, he stated that everybody at the bureau was still working. "He either lied or he didn't know," Dodd-Ramirez concluded. In fact, like so many other federal workers, the hundreds of investigators and economists and lawyers and consumer advocates were in essence being paid to twiddle their thumbs. Meanwhile, investigations into predatory lending went undone and ordinary consumers found they had one less institution in their corner in DC. "I'm not allowed to reach out to external parties," the CFPB staffer explained. "Everyone's supposed to be working, but no one is."

For 24-year-old Carmen Drier (not their real name), the job they had snagged out west, at the Department of the Interior's US Geological Survey was a dream come true.

Originally from New Jersey, Carmen had graduated from Rutgers State University with an Environmental Geography degree. They had first come out as a lesbian after Trump was elected in 2016, and, now, in 2025 — with the flurry of Executive Orders and government policy shifts against use of the "they/them" pronouns on official documents and government emails — had decided to adopt the gender-neutral pronouns as a form of personal protest against the cascading intolerance emanating out of DC. "I was like, 'Fuck this. If you're really going to be a dick about it, this is who I am.' It feels more comfortable now to use it in my daily life." They had thought of adding the pronouns to their official work email just to show how angry the Executive Orders made them feel — but ultimately decided not to do anything that could bring more federal wrath down on their colleagues.

Carmen was an idealist. Out of college, they had worked as a volunteer with AmeriCorps, in Colorado. When that work began to wind down, in the spring of 2024, they decided to apply for government jobs.

Carmen Drier wanted to make an impact on how regions prepared for climate change, and at the time government work for a recent graduate with an itch to do good by the environment seemed a no-brainer. The government had the resources to collate the necessary data on climate change, and there was room for a data-person such as Drier to find their niche and make the difference they so desperately wanted to make. By August of 2024, Carmen was working for the feds, an entry-level data manager at the Department of the Interior's US Geological Survey. When the scientists at the center, many of whom had been there for longer than Carmen had been alive, came up with new data on forest growth, on endangered species, on wildfire risks, it was the 24-year-old's job to get that information out to the public.

For the first few months, things seemed to be going smoothly. The work was interesting, there was no dress code — they could show up to work in blue jeans, turned up at the ankles, flowery shirts, and heavy work boots. And, perhaps more to the point, it was important: the team was developing information, usable in real time, that could protect communities from the sorts of forest mega-fires that had scorched millions of acres and devastated the West over the past decade. That more than made up for the mediocre pay — their starting salary was a mere $54,000, which would have made paying the monthly bills a stretch had it not been for the fact they had lucked out and found a single room in a sprawling ranch house out in the suburbs, with a large garden complete with a barbeque and an orange tree.

But then came the inauguration. The old guard, led by Secretary of the Interior Deb Haaland, the country's first-ever Native American Secretary of the Interior, was out, and a new guard, seemingly more concerned with raiding the public lands for as much private profit as was possible, was in. Things started to go south pretty quickly.

First, the center's employees got an email explaining to them that all DEI programs and employees related to those programs were being rooted out — and, perhaps even more concerning, that employees were being ordered to report colleagues who might surreptitiously be continuing on with DEI-related projects. It seemed the sort of government-mandated snitching policy that might have been encouraged in the old Soviet Union and its satellite states, or in Putin's Russia or Xi's China, not something that one would expect in the United States. Then, hot on the heels of this noxious missive, came the DOGE-inspired Fork In The Road letters urging Drier and their colleagues to take a deferred resignation offer and to find themselves "more productive" work outside of government. With the writing on the wall, more and more of the scientists and their support staff opted to take the deferred resignation, going onto Administrative Leave and looking for other jobs. As they did so, scientific projects, some of them decades in the making, got pushed aside, or rushed to premature conclusions. And for those USGS staffers who remained, the work load ratcheted up as they tried to plug the gaps left by the departure of their colleagues. In some units of the agency, by early spring one in four workers would have decided to call it quits.

Finally, on Valentine's Day the firings began.

Drier wasn't at work that day — they had just switched over to a compressed work schedule. But their cell phone was still on, and that was how they heard, from a colleague, that people were losing their jobs. Everything seemed chaotic, the colleague told them; their boss didn't know what was happening, all anyone seemed to know was that an awful lot of people were being told to turn in their computers and their cell phones and to leave the buildings in which they had worked. Four days later, when Drier returned to work after the weekend, that morning their boss called them on a video chat and told them that, as a probationary worker, they were being fired. Their work would end at the close of business that day, at which point they would hand in their computer and have to leave the premises. As a probationary employee, they weren't entitled to any severance pay — though they did have their annual leave left, which when paid out as cash would come to roughly $1,100. It was enough to pay their bills for a week, maybe two — and then, well, if they were honest with themself, they didn't exactly know what they would do.

"I was in a car crash when I was a teenager. I rate all of my fear against that one moment," Carmen Drier explained. "It [being fired] wasn't as bad as that. But it was definitely a gut-dropping moment. I was very proud of myself. I didn't cry at work. But I came home and went roller skating, gay night at the rink downtown. Made coconut pudding, and ate it with my roommate — and cried with her."

This wasn't the start to their work life that Drier had envisioned. It made them feel jaded — which was a strange feeling for someone so young and so innately idealistic. It made them suspicious of the federal government, and even made them hesitant about applying for state jobs — though, as the winter wore on they would find themselves, along with many of their colleagues, at job fairs looking for work with California state agencies. After all, California's Governor Newsom had said that California was in the market to pick up skilled scientists and other federal workers who had run afoul of Musk's chainsaw tactics.

* * *

On balance, though, it seemed a safer bet to beat a strategic retreat. Drier decided to head back east, and to return to their parents' house while they regrouped and charted out a new chapter. They were young and, they noted, relatively footloose — no mortgage, the possibility of falling back on their parents' health insurance, no long-term relationship tying them to one place. So why not make a road trip adventure of the whole thing?

Drier decided to pack their life's possessions into boxes, stick them in the back of their old Honda Fit, and map out a meandering, two-week, journey back to their parents' house in suburban New Jersey. It felt weird; almost like when they had returned home from college at the start of the Covid pandemic, when everything shut down and all their classes went virtual. Like slipping back into childhood again after making strides into adulthood. They canvassed their friends for suggested playlists to listen to during the long days of driving, "alt-folk metal stuff," Drier explained, and did a series of farewell visits with people they cared about who were dotted around the region.

The visits dulled the pain somewhat, but still, Drier couldn't shake the feeling of fury that had been gnawing at them ever since the firings began. And, because they had virtually no control over the events that were unfolding, that rage had begun to curdle. "I feel like if I'm angry about something, in order to feel okay about it I want to have some control over what happens next. And this feels like a hurricane came through and tore everything up. I was in the path of something bigger."

That their life could have been turned upside down simply on the whim of someone like Elon Musk horrified them. Musk, they felt, was a "very ridiculous man." They wanted to ask him about what he had missed in life to make him turn out that way.

Like Drier, Ed Brisbane (not his real name) was just beginning his career. He and his identical twin brother had both graduated from Central Washington University in 2024, both with majors in economics, and they had jointly decided to apply for federal employment afterwards.

The young men, tall, large boned, with a shock of mouse-brown hair parted slightly to the left, had grown up just outside of Buckley, Washington, a speck of a town with a few thousand residents, half an hour's drive from Mount Rainier. It was the sort of place where, when a new McDonald's franchise opened up, it was big news. Weekends, Ed would hang with his friends, or go on long trail runs — he was on his high school's track and cross-country teams. Beyond that, there really wasn't much to do.

Buckley's politics trended red, as did Ed's family. They were instinctually anti-tax; believed that the word "bureaucrat" was a synonym for wasteful government spending; were suspicious of foreign aid; and knew exactly where they stood on hot-button culture war issues. Ed's father had voted for Trump in 2016, and had he not died a few years later, would, his son noted, have almost certainly supported him again in 2020 and 2024. Ed's mother was less politically vocal, but Ed was pretty sure that she, too, had, on more than one occasion, cast her ballot for the MAGA movement's leader.

Ed himself had been too young to vote in 2016; hadn't navigated the mail-in voting process during the Covid-year election of 2020; and, in 2024, had been so unenthusiastic about both candidates that he had sat that election out too. But, in local and state races, he cast his lot with Republicans. He had been watching a lot of Joe Rogan recently, liked most of his politics — though thought he overdid it in his undiluted enthusiasm for Elon Musk and Donald Trump — and was a fan of his macho persona, especially his frequent discussion of weightlifting. Ed's regimen involved going to the gym to pump iron at least five days a week. During Covid, Ed had become increasingly uncomfortable with what he saw as the censorship of outside-the-box thinking on the pandemic and how to respond to it. And, he said, as a young white man he was turned off by how often Democrats reached for the "racist" or "sexist" label as a way to shut down political debate. "You say something, people get cancelled," he argued.

Somewhat sheltered and without too much of a sense of the world outside of the United States — he had only been out of the country once, on a high school trip to southern Spain, though he, his twin brother, and a bunch of high school buddies were planning, and saving up for, a second trip, this time to Germany — he wanted little more than security. In the spring of 2024, an IRS job in Seattle opened up, one that involved talking on the phone to taxpayers all day every day about their outstanding balances and ways they could pay off moneys owed the government, and, despite his family's engrained suspicion of big government and high taxation, Ed applied. The pay was mediocre — on the government pay scale he would start off at a mere $44,000 — but it did offer both the prospect of safe employment and also of steady salary raises; and, since his brother was also seeking federal work in western Washington, they would be able to share an apartment together, as they had done in university, and stretch their rent money. That wasn't something to sneeze at in a part of the country where rents had been spiraling upwards in recent years.

Ed Brisbane began working for the IRS in the late spring, on the twentieth floor of a downtown federal building. He and his brother would set their alarms for 6:15 a.m., in their sparse apartment, its walls devoid of any decoration, in a large complex several miles south of the airport, have a quick breakfast, and head to the station to catch the 7 a.m. train. Each day, from 8 a.m. onwards, Ed spent upwards of seven hours on the phones. Because the work involved dealing with highly personal information — social security numbers, tax ID numbers, and so on — the workers were carefully tracked. Brisbane thought he was being "micro-managed." It wasn't always fun, but he was good at the job and enjoyed the fact there was a gym on the third floor of the building that he could use after work each day. In January 2025, he got a positive performance review.

The review, it turned out, wasn't worth the paper it was written on. As the DOGE purges got underway days later, Brisbane's IRS office was hit, and the 24-year-old, as an employee with three months of his probationary period left, received the generic letter informing him he was being fired for poor performance. "No severance pay. They just gave us an hour or two to clean out our desks," he recalled. Neither Brisbane nor his colleagues could access information from the government about what was happening; instead they had to turn to social media, getting snippets of information from Reddit feeds and other sites. Their access to team chats on Microsoft was immediately cut off, their email addresses deactivated. For Brisbane, who had at first been willing to give Trump the benefit of the doubt when he heard the new president discussing cutting government payrolls, it was a powerful, and brutal, lesson in *realpolitik*. "I don't know why anyone would want to work for the government again," he concluded. "There's no protection. They can get away with whatever they want."

It took a full week for his formal termination letter to arrive in the mail. Each day that he waited for the letter to arrive made him angrier. He would scroll the Reddit threads that he was on, spending hours reading up on the stories of fired workers in one agency after the next, and also reading about the administration's increasingly aggressive attacks on judges who tried to slow the carnival of cuts down. Like a lightbulb going on, he realized that this wasn't simply about trimming the fat off of a bloated system. "I'm seeing all the essential things they're cutting," he admitted. "I didn't think they meant firing a ton of people and going after the courts."

* * *

Suddenly, those courts seemed to him to be his last, best hope for a semblance of fairness. And, true to form, two weeks later, in the face of court orders reinstating at least some of the fired employees in at least some of the eviscerated agencies, Brisbane's job was reactivated and he was put back on the IRS's payroll.

But, like so many other fired-and-then-rehired employees, he was forbidden from actually doing any work. In a truly Kafka-esque move, the federal government told people like Brisbane to stay at home in order to keep receiving their paycheck. And so, he did. He received backpay for the weeks in which he had been fired; and he received paychecks and benefits for doing nothing. It made no sense — the length of time callers to the IRS were being placed on hold was skyrocketing since there were so many fewer staff available to answer calls — but there was nothing Brisbane could do about it. "You'd think they'd want to bring us back to make more revenue — because more IRS agents mean more revenue for the government," he mused. "But they don't want that, obviously. It doesn't make sense."

Stuck in this DOGE-imposed purgatory between work and no-work, Brisbane decided to rustle up his high school crew and finally go on that German trip they had been fantasizing about for so many years. "It's kind of funny; they're paying me to go on vacation!" he exclaimed, reveling in the absurdity of it all. This was how Elon Musk's cleanup crew intended to save the American taxpayers' money. "Germany for ten days, with my friends."

In Cincinnati, Ohio, Hannah Echt was also experiencing a sense of unreality about what was happening in the country. For she, too, had been doing vital work and then had been ordered to simply stop.

Growing up, Echt didn't have the usual career-dreams of her contemporaries. She didn't want to be an influencer, or a firefighter, she had no desires to be a music star or an astronaut... But she did very much want to be an occupational safety expert, as had been her father before her. She had seen the difference that he had made, and wanted to follow in his footsteps.

In the mid-oughts, Echt studied anthropology at Kenyon College, a liberal arts campus 160 miles northeast of her hometown. During her winter and summer breaks, she bounced around different offices of the National Institute for Occupational Safety and Health (NIOSH) — an agency under the auspices of the Department of Health & Human Services established in 1970 under the same legislation that created the better-known OSHA. The work fascinated her — and it was because of it that she decided to go to graduate school, applying for, and getting accepted into, a master's program in occupational hygiene at the University of Washington's Seattle campus. She recognized that it wasn't necessarily the sexiest of degrees, and most people likely had no idea what the term even meant — basically, it involved identifying and then finding ways to ameliorate workplace hazards so as to protect the workforce, and, depending on the hazard, the surrounding community — but she was passionate about workplace safety. In the summer of 2019, while she was finishing up her degree, she got an internship with the Public Health Service, as a Junior Commissioned Officer Student Training and Eastern Program (JCOSTEP). The acronym was clunky, but the work was, for Echt, a once-in-a-lifetime opportunity. The public health service would place her with a federal agency that met her specialty skillset, and Echt pushed hard for that placement to be with NIOSH.

That was how Hannah Echt ended up working at the agency full-time— in a subunit named the Health Hazard Evaluation Program. HHEP had something of an open-door approach; employers aware of potential problems in their workplaces could call, asking for help. But, at the same time, so could employees, or their unions, if they worried that their bosses weren't addressing their safety concerns. Unlike OSHA, HHEP didn't have punitive powers; it couldn't slap fines on wayward employers or force compliance with codes — but it could, and did, have the ability to call on a slew of safety experts from around the country, epidemiologists, doctors, occupational nurses, support staff, to work out how best to ameliorate dangerous conditions. It was a fair bet that, without these interventions, many more workers would become disabled, or even die, as a result of exposure to toxins and other dangers.

When, a few months later, in the darkest early days of the Covid pandemic, she graduated from University of Washington, rather than try to reinvent her wheel Echt applied to NIOSH for a full-time job. After all, she was a known quantity there and had already demonstrated her proficiency in mitigating dangers in the workplace.

Later that summer, after she had gone through the time-consuming application process, gotten her security clearance, and done all the paperwork, she was formally offered a job. In October, she reported for work, as what was known as a Title 42 Fellow, meaning her initial contract was for three years, with an expectation that, if she performed up to par, it would roll over for another three years, and so on. It didn't, however, come with employment guarantees; under the terms of the Title 42 contract, its fellows could be fired at any time.

Given the scale of loss that Covid was inflicting in the autumn of 2020, NIOSH had limited in-person work, and so the job would start off with her working remotely; but she hoped that, over time, normalcy would return and she would again be able to spend her days in the Health Hazard Evaluation Program offices, in her home town of Cincinnati. For many reasons, most of them involving family, that prospect made her happy; she had two older siblings, and both had flown the roost, one living out in the suburbs, another in Rhode Island — and her parents were delighted by the idea that she, at least, would be returning to Cincinnati to start her career. That she was doing a job so close to her father's heart added to the sense of accomplishment. She was, too, in a long-term relationship, and her boyfriend was also rooted to the city. How wonderful, they thought, that they could begin their professional lives in a place they both loved, that they could think about starting their own family in a few years knowing that both sets of grandparents would be living nearby.

* * *

The work was exciting. One day, the managers of a pharmaceuticals company might call NIOSH, worried that workers at their plant were being exposed to high levels of pharmaceutical dust. Another day, they might get a request about poor air quality in a factory. Or they might have to visit a cannabis processing facility to understand ventilation risks. Or they might go to a drywall-processing facility to see how best to tamp down exposure to dangerous small particulate matter. Echt and her colleagues would plan site visits and do what they called "desktop investigations," involving interviews of all the relevant players, checking OSHA logs, sampling air quality. There was more than an element of the detective in her job, and it gave her great pleasure when she was able to come up with recommendations that would make workers safer. She felt valued; spread around the country, in offices in DC, Ohio, West Virginia, Alaska, Pennsylvania, Washington, Georgia and Colorado, NIOSH had approximately 1,300 employees, but it only had a few dozen employees, in Cincinnati and in Morgantown, West Virginia, who did the type of investigative work that she did. The Ohio office had a reputation for being generalist — picking up any-and-every workplace safety investigation; the West Virginia office specialized in respiratory hazards facing coal miners.

Below the radar, NIOSH was doing vital work. It had established a national firefighter registry for cancer exploring the risks that firefighters faced for developing a slew of cancers because of the toxins they were exposed to on the job. Ironically, given Donald Trump's subsequent turn against the agency, it had been Trump himself who, in 2018, signed the legislation creating the registry. As of March of 2025, when it stopped accepting new enrollees, the firefighters' registry had enrolled 24,000 firefighters. NIOSH had also set up a program to identify the health challenges faced by first responders at the World Trade Center following the terrorist attacks of September 11, 2001. It ran a lab that certified respiratory equipment used by firefighters and coal miners. It had created a national surveillance program to monitor coal miners for a range of work-related diseases. It also helped train industrial hygienists out in the community to replicate some of the research NIOSH teams were doing. Being a part of all of this filled Echt with pride. There was, quite simply, no other agency in the country doing this work. On a shoestring budget, the agency was saving lives and helping people with chronic lung diseases, cancers, and other workplace-related ailments, get the help that they needed. It was hard to imagine work that was more important to the public interest.

And then DOGE's chainsaw descended on the agency. Days after Trump was inaugurated, even before the broader cuts to the federal workforce got underway, Echt and all the other Title 42 fellows at NIOSH were informed that their contracts would not be renewed when their three years were up. Ten weeks later, on March 31, upwards of 80 percent of NIOSH's employees were informed that they would be fired at the end of June as part of the agency's Reduction In Force, and all of its administrators were promptly placed on Administrative Leave. The letter Echt received from Tom Nagy, Health & Human Services Chief Human Capital Officer, was, to say the least, tone-deaf. "We recognize the valuable contributions of all our employees and deeply regret the need to take this action. Our priority is to ensure a fair and transparent process while providing the necessary support to those affected." It concluded, "Thank you for your understanding and cooperation during this challenging time." And with that, in all-but-name, NIOSH, one of the most successful workplace safety agencies in the country's history, was being demolished.

For Echt, who agreed to speak to me for the research for this book in her capacity as an AFGE union member and steward, it meant that her life plans had been shredded. She and her boyfriend were planning to get married, and now, if the RIF held and the agency was destroyed, they didn't know where her income would come from, where'd they'd be living, whether they'd be able to stay near their parents or would have to move hundreds, maybe thousands of miles away for new employment.

The industrial hygienist couldn't fathom how she and her colleagues were being treated — and how the men and women whose health depended on their work were simply being cast to one side as if they were garbage. She looked at what the federal government was doing and saw it as "kind of like a big F U for everything. A lot of us wanted to work in these jobs because we wanted a job in public service. They're not even saying 'thank you,' they're saying 'you're done. Get a real job.' They don't even understand what we do. It doesn't feel like any thought went into this. We're all just names on a spreadsheet and an algorithm spewed out who to cut."

Weeks after he had been fired from one of the country's premier scientific agencies, Charlie Wright (not his real name) was also struggling with the mental health side-effects.

Wright had bills to pay — two young kids enrolled in private school, a mortgage. His wife had been out of the workforce since the children were born. And he felt the weight of the world upon his shoulders. He was looking for new jobs, but, so far, nothing had panned out. He was hoping he would be re-hired by the Feds, but at the moment all he had to cling to were the rumors swirling around on social media and in chat groups, made up of fired federal workers, that he was part of. Some people were saying the courts would force the Trump people to bring the fired probationary workers back; some were saying the last couple of months were simply the chaotic first steps of a new Administration trying to find its footing — and that, when the dust settled, things would be ok for most of the federal workforce. Others tended apocalyptic, talking about everything almost in End Times terms.

Wright had spent the past few decades conducting critical research for the government in fisheries up and down the coasts, as well as charting atmospheric activity. He had a skill-set that few others in the world possessed. Now, however, he was out of work, for what he considered to be an entirely non-sensical reason — having shifted jobs shortly before the new

Administration took power, he was considered a probationary worker, and, in consequence, he had been culled in the great purges of mid-February. There hadn't been any attempt at common sense, nor any effort to account for the fact that he was a middle-aged man with a generation's worth of experience at the agency from which he was now being fired; he had, he realized, simply become "a name on a spreadsheet, just like everyone else. I was put on the chopping block." It was the sort of kick in the guts that could, he now saw, fell a man.

On Reddit threads, he and others shared their fury. He dreamed of going into electoral politics to get his revenge, of taking down via the ballot box at least one of the MAGA representatives from his state. He wanted to scream from the rooftops that the government had invested millions of dollars in his research and in his salary over the decades and now, to meet Elon Musk's body-count demands, was simply throwing it all away. Talk about a waste of taxpayer dollars.

"Anxiety and depression clearly caught me," he admitted. He found it hard to face his family each day, was obsessed with how to pay the household's bills. "I don't want to face the world right now," he announced. "I want to stay home and not talk to anybody. I'm angry. I can't watch the news. I feel like I'm going through the five stages of grief."

A veteran, Wright had eventually reached out to the VA for counselling. Their teams had, he said, gotten back to him pretty quickly; they seemed like they cared. But he hadn't yet started talking to a professional about what was going on in his head. He felt that he was traumatized, and what made it all so much worse, he was convinced that his own government had deliberately set out to inflict that trauma on the thousands of federal workers it was firing. After all, the way they were being let go was nothing short of a public beat-down. Despite all the years he had put into public service, all the vital scientific research he had done that had helped farmers, fishermen, and countless other around the country, he now felt completely unvalued. "You get nothing out of it," he said bitterly of the decades of work he had put in. "Except a kick in the ass on the way out. It's so imprinted on my brain that I'll never forget this; and I'll always speak up about it. You can compare it to a traumatic event in your life. Losing somebody. I feel like I'm losing twenty years of pouring my heart and soul into the agency and not being appreciated anymore. This was a life for me. That's the trauma part. I gave so much of myself to this, and to have it tossed away and thrown aside; it's very real."

The tension was palpable in Wright's house. His wife was also anxious; and his kids, aged seven and eleven, had grasped the fact that the family was in a bad way. They, too, felt scared, and that, their father acknowledged, broke his heart.

"This whole situation bled over to my family life, friends, neighbors, everything," Wright admitted. Some days, when he was feeling particularly bleak, he felt "like there's no tomorrow." Oftentimes, he woke up in the middle of the night, unable to sleep, counting down the minutes until the local swimming pool opened and he could put in a fierce hour or more of fast swimming to banish the morning's jitters. He had taken to wearing a baseball cap with a logo from his agency around town, taking solace from the words of support that community members would give him. Somehow, their kindness made him feel slightly better. But even that was a double-edged sword. The moment he started to melt a little, he felt vulnerable, felt that he was setting himself up for another fall. "At 48 years old, you'd think I would be a tough cookie," he explained. "But it really sucks."

Like Hannah Echt, Dan Meleason had grown up in Ohio. He had attended Ohio State University, taking his sweet time to work out what he wanted to study, and, eventually, after six years, had graduated with a BA in political science. He had, during those years, joined the Navy ROTC and it rapidly became more than a side-show for him; it was, rather, a passion. The day he graduated, in late August 2001, less than two weeks before the 9/11 terrorist attacks, he was commissioned; he would spend the next twenty-one years of his life in the Navy.

Meleason had wanted, initially, to become either a pilot or a SEAL. But his physical showed that he had a form of astigmatism that wasn't correctable by surgery, and his commanding officer took the young graduate aside and bluntly told him that he would never qualify either as a pilot or a SEAL. It was devastating. "I felt my professional life was crumbling in front of me," Meleason remembered, a generation on. It wasn't. In fact, with hindsight, the astigmatism diagnosis might have been a blessing in disguise. Instead of bundling him off to train as a pilot, Meleason's commanding officer recommended that he train as a cryptologist, gave him some books to read on cryptography, and then sent him off for four months of training at the Corry Station naval training center in Pensacola, Florida.

With the War on Terror remaking American foreign policy and military priorities, skilled cryptologists were in particularly high demand. Meleason was sent to Oahu, Hawaii, a three-year posting that had him on land occasionally and deployed on submarines for weeks at a time more frequently. Basically, he said, only half-joking, he would return to the island every so often to "pay some bills, get some sun, do some surfing," and then he'd deploy back underwater again.

Over the two decades that followed, the cryptography specialist would rotate into different postings around the country: to Fort Gordon, Georgia; to Fort Meade, Maryland; to Virginia Beach; to Colorado Springs; and finally back, again, to Fort Meade. Somewhere along the way, he managed to complete an MBA at the University of North Carolina.

* * *

Meleason rose up the ranks and felt that he was making a difference. He served in combat locations in various locales around the world and took part in senior planning meetings in DC and elsewhere around shifting transnational threats. At times, he intuited that he was getting a sneak-peak behind the scenes, seeing "the world as it really, truly works." It wasn't all pretty; and when Donald Trump won the Electoral College vote in 2016 and became president in early 2017, Meleason felt that it had suddenly become even less pretty. He grew increasingly worried about Trump's rhetoric, concerned that the military would be ordered to do illegal acts — and he became preoccupied about the likelihood of international blowback. He was worried about Russian involvement in the 2016 election — and, again, in 2020, during the pandemic. The MAGA presidency, he realized, was "crushing my soul. I was trying to do good work with international partners and being stymied by him and his administration." When the events of January 6, 2021, unfolded with Trump egging on a violent crowd intent on preventing Congress from certifying his electoral defeat, it was, for Meleason, "the straw that broke the proverbial camel's back."

Months later, with the twenty years under his belt that would secure him a decent military pension and after long heart-to-hearts with his partner about what to do, he decided to retire and look for federal work as a civilian. It was a time-consuming process. In his mid-forties, and with a military pension that gave him something of a financial cushion, he didn't want to take just any job. It had to be something he really cared about. Finally, living in Colorado and wanting to work with nature, in the spring of 2023 he applied for two open positions at the US Forest Service, which was a part of the US Department of Agriculture, and ended up accepting one as a Partnership Coordinator, working with individuals and organizations in the community to mitigate the risk of fires both in forests and in grasslands.

In March, 2024, the erstwhile cryptologist was on-boarded, after a months' long process, at a salary only about two-thirds of what he had made when he retired from the navy; and, wanting to hit the ground running, he immediately began working long days — days that would often stretch out into nights — putting together strategies to protect the region from fires. With climate change accelerating, the area was particularly vulnerable; four of the five largest fires in Colorado history had occurred within the past few years, and all twenty of the state's largest conflagrations had occurred since the start of the century.

Twice a week, Meleason would be in the Forest Service's Pueblo office, in the high desert that stretches eastward from the edge of the Rockies in southern Colorado and out into the Great Plains. The rest of the time, he'd be driving all over Colorado and Kansas, meeting with locals to strategize about how to mitigate fire risk. Oftentimes, his contacts, tired after a long day of working their farms, would want to meet him in their homes, and he would always accommodate, driving sometimes hundreds of miles, and then patiently waiting until they had finished their dinners with their families. Only then, at 7, or 8, or 9 p.m., would he sit down with them and talk shop. It was exhausting work, but it was also just what Meleason wanted. He was helping preserve the landscape he loved, and helping protect the community in a part of the country that he now thought of as home.

* * *

Then, to Meleason's horror — though not, he claimed, to his surprise — Trump was elected again. In late 2024, 713,000 military veterans were employed in civilian roles by the federal government. Months later, in the frantic weeks following the inauguration, tens of thousands of those veterans would suddenly find themselves in DOGE's firing line, many of them, like Meleason, having only recently entered the civilian workforce after decades in the military and thus being categorized as newbies, as disposable probationary employees.

By late February, a month into the new presidency, upwards of 6,000 veterans had already lost their federal jobs. And that was just the beginning: The Department of Veterans Affairs alone was slated to shed upwards of 80,000 positions as part of a downsizing effort over the coming years — about 20,000 of which were jobs held by veterans. Numerous grants to programs aimed at helping veterans with housing, healthcare, substance abuse treatment, and so on, were being cut. And across the federal government waves of layoffs, many of which were impacting veterans, were breaking, one after the next after the next.

Meleason was amongst those who early on felt the wrong end of the DOGE stick. On February 13, shortly after lunch, his supervisor phoned him and told him he was being fired. "Even though," the Navy vet noted, "I had that whole veteran's background, had vets preference, and only had one month left on my probationary status. It was heartbreaking."

Trump had claimed, on the campaign trail during three presidential elections, that he was the candidate who best understood and most cared for veterans; he had, repeatedly, wrapped himself in the flag and posited himself as the military man's best friend. On hot mics, he was less complimentary, using crude language to denigrate those who were wounded or died while in uniform, and mocking prisoners of war such as his onetime GOP nemesis John McCain. He reportedly told advisors that he didn't want to be photographed with wounded vets because their disfigurements would ruin the photographs. Now, under his watch, thousands of veterans were being dismissed from government jobs and virtually frog-marched out of their offices.

Because Meleason was a probationary employee, he received no severance pay. His health insurance and other benefits were also terminated — though, for him, since his navy retirement came with health coverage, the loss of these benefits was less important. His heart bled, however, for so many others who didn't have this added layer of protection. He felt that no-one in a position of authority had gone to bat for him, or for his colleagues, that they had essentially left him alone on the battlefield against a vastly better-armed foe, and that the USDA bigwigs, secure in their Beltway jobs, "didn't fight the good fight. It was a shock, a letdown."

* * *

Dan Meleason did what he always did when the going got tough: He sought out a way to burn off all the adrenalin, all the anger and the frustration. At 6 a.m. the next morning, he grabbed his old Armada JJ skis, he and a buddy packed up one of their cars, and they headed to the ski resort of Breckenridge, a two and a half hour drive up into the Rockies. "We skied twenty runs," Meleason remembered. Ski down the mountain, head back up again on a lift; ski down the mountain, head back up again on a lift. "We were skiing really hard." When they finally called it a day, at 3:30 p.m., they were both exhausted. It was, he decided, a good routine to get into.

Over the coming months, as he attempted to navigate the new terrain that he found himself on, Meleason would ski a lot. He would also go hiking. And he would also, many, many times over the coming weeks, click onto LinkedIn, hoping that something would leap out at him and whisper the outlines of the next chapter in his life.

PART TWO

RE-HIRES AND RIFS

In early April, Ed Brisbane, his brother, four of their male high school friends, and two of the guys' girlfriends, flew out to Berlin. They had been planning the trip for months, since shortly after the election, and Ed had been saving some of his not particularly large pay check each month for the overseas splurge.

The ex-IRS worker wasn't particularly well-traveled. Apart from that one trip to Spain back when he was in high school, when the class had gone to Malaga and Seville, he'd never been abroad. But he had studied about World War II and he was fascinated by the history. Ted and his friends plotted a whirlwind itinerary that involved numerous train rides and would allow them to see many of Germany's great cities and also take a zag over to Prague.

The group flew overnight, arriving in Berlin on April 5. They were planning to spend two nights in the capital city, cramming is as many museums and historic sites as possible. From there, they were going to head to Dresden; south to Prague; and back into Germany to visit Heidelberg, Munich, and a few other cities.

On a bus early in their trip, they overhead a middle-aged German guy making fun of Trump. He realized the group were Americans and enthusiastically gave them the middle finger. It was a peculiarly intimate statement of growing global distaste for America; an Ipsos poll released in mid-April showed that in

26 of the 29 countries polled, an increasing number of people felt the US had a negative impact on world affairs. In Canada, a country that Trump had repeatedly denigrated, saying that it ought to be absorbed into the US as its 51st state, only 19 percent had a positive view of the US's role on the global stage. These numbers represented an astounding collapse in global confidence in what had, until recently, widely been seen as the country that anchored global stability. Ted and his friends were too happy in their travels to care. As they realized they had just, collectively, been given the bird, they all started laughing.

* * *

The six weeks following Brisbane's firing from the IRS had been nerve-racking. All over the country, judges were hearing lawsuits, some of which would make their way up to the Supreme Court, against the dismantling of government agencies without congressional approval and the wholesale firing of probationary staff. A tug-of-war was underway around Executive power and whether Trump had the right to completely ignore Congressionally-passed laws establishing these agencies, or Congressionally-approved funding to keep these agencies running. Depending on the day and the latest court ruling, it would either appear as though Trump could get away with anything or that soon the fired workers would be ordered back to work *en masse.* For the workers themselves, it was a nail-biting time: Would they get their jobs back and be paid back-pay, or would the courts give their imprimatur on the firing process? Ed had no idea how it would all play out — and he hoped to be able to at least partially put aside all of the stress until he returned from his vacation.

Meanwhile, after shaking off the torpor and disbelief that for so many progressives had characterized those first, fearful weeks, protestors were now taking to the streets of cities large and small in protest at the actions of Trump and of DOGE. Pretty much every day, one group or another was protesting, occupying buildings, disrupting traffic on highways. Outside Tesla salesrooms most Saturdays, as winter gave way to spring, crowds would gather, loudly making known their displeasure with Elon Musk and urging passing drivers to honk their support for the demonstrators. Trump had responded by demanding courts consider protestors — especially those who vandalized cars and showrooms — as domestic terrorists. It was an ominous threat, made more so given that he had also labeled purported Venezuelan gang members as terrorists and had had military aircraft fly nearly 300 of them to El Salvador, where they were promptly put into the CECOT super-max prison, there to be held indefinitely. Trump was musing aloud now about the possibility of also sending US citizens convicted of certain offenses to that same god-awful prison.

Two days before Ed Brisbane left for Europe, the IRS announced that, in order to comply with the latest court rulings, it would be reinstating all 7,000 of the probationary workers it had fired back in February. They would, the letter announced, soon be receiving instructions on how to return to full-time work on April 14, the day before the deadline for filing 2024 tax returns. Ed was going to still be in Europe, but now he had a job to return to when he got back and, more importantly, backpay to look forward to.

Of course, that job would likely not last long — the Administration had already made it clear it was only accepting the court's orders reluctantly, and IRS leadership was already looking for ways to implement a Reduction-In-Force, the technical term used for a systematic down-sizing of the scale of a federal agency or department. One day the IRS workers would be told they were going to return to their offices; the next day they'd be told they weren't expected to come in. Nobody seemed to know anything, and those higher up the food chain seemed so worried about their own jobs that they weren't paying attention to what was happening lower down. Rumors were also circulating that federal workers were going to start receiving a whole new set of missives pressuring them to accept deferred resignations — which would basically give them a few months of salary in exchange for them not working and then, come the summer, parting ways with their federal jobs.

Ed, who ran nervous, now realized he had something else to worry about as he embarked on his European adventure.

* * *

The evening of April 9 was a busy one. Ed and his friends were in Prague, all of them staying in one large room in an Airbnb on the river's edge west of the city center. They had gone on a bit of a bender that night, heading out to a restaurant that put on a five-course "Medieval Dinner," the not particularly imaginative centerpiece of which was chicken legs. The main show was a guy and a gal dancing around on stage with swords, while off to the side belly dancers strutted their stuff. There was a jester, too, and juggling. It wasn't bad — though, truth be told, he'd seen a better Medieval-themed show once in Disneyland. What made it more exciting was that there was an all-you-can-drink bar, so Ed and his friends had made a point of downing as many Pilsner beers as they could.

Sometime that night, during the revelry, Ed had checked his email and seen that the Supreme Court had, the previous day, ruled against his union and given the okay for IRS workers to be fired again. It was all too much; as they got nearer to the Airbnb, so Ed's stress levels went stratospheric. And then, to cap it all, there it was on his email: Another letter urging him to take Deferred Resignation.

Perhaps it was the beers thinking for him, but late that night, as his friends drifted off to sleep around him, Ed Brisbane realized he wanted out: The stress of not knowing whether he would have a job the next day had become simply too much for him; it was threatening to swamp him. In his inebriated state, he turned on his phone's roaming feature so that he could receive an ID.ME verification text that would allow him to reply to the deferred resignation offer, and, before he knew it, he had sent back an email expressing "interest in the offer." It would be two weeks before he got the terms of that offer in the mail, but when, eventually, they arrived, after he had returned Stateside, the letter containing them informed Brisbane that he would be working with his unit of the agency for a couple months and would, after that, be placed on Administrative Leave for three more months. In other words, like so many other federal workers, he was being ordered to sit on his ass and do nothing in exchange for his salary. He was encouraged to seek out additional employment, even though he already had, at least for now, one federal job, and decided to increase the number of hours he was working as a cruise ship check-in agent (he'd previously been employed there weekends to bring in additional cash). Setting aside the value of his government job's benefits, the base hourly salary from the cruise line job was nearly four dollars per hour higher than it had been at the IRS.

Brisbane felt entirely disillusioned by what the federal government had done over the prior weeks. "I'm pretty pissed and upset, for sure," he said. "I'm pretty pissed at Elon Musk; pretty upset with the courts as well. This government hasn't helped me all. I've lost faith in it for sure."

The probationary staff at the CDC, it turned out, ended up having it better than did many of their peers in other government agencies.

Shortly after they were all fired, ostensibly for poor performance, they were informed that they would be placed on paid Administrative Leave for four weeks, meaning that they would have an income even while they were forbidden to work. Then, in late February, in response to a lawsuit filed by several trade unions representing government workers, US District Judge William Alsup ruled that the Office of Personnel Management had exceeded its authority in ordering several government agencies to fire their probationary workers, and temporarily blocked their dismissal.

Aryn Backus and Adrian M were told their Administrative Leave would be extended by a week. Then it was extended another week beyond that. And finally it was extended indefinitely, until all of the court cases had resolved. Another judge ruled that the government agencies had until May 8 to either submit proof that their fired employees had, indeed, exhibited poor performance at work or to submit a new termination letter informing them that poor performance wasn't really the reason they had been fired.

For Backus, the time off work turned out to be something of a godsend. She was receiving her full salary but wasn't allowed into the CDC offices, a situation that, as a taxpayer, she recognized made literally no sense. And so, she spent her time organizing protests and campaigns against the government cuts — she co-founded a group called Fired But Fighting; visited her sister in coastal Florida; and traveled with her husband on his work trips. She went to yoga classes and perused employment ads. She had applied for several public health jobs but hadn't snagged any interviews. It was hard, she recognized; first off, she was competing with hundreds of other fired CDC workers; and second, so many federal public health grants to states and cities and non-profits were on hold that almost no-one was hiring. Vast parts of the country's patchwork quilt public health infrastructure had gone into deep freeze.

"It's crazy; I would love to work," she acknowledged. "I love my job. I'd rather be doing it. But instead, I'm being paid to not do anything. It's crazy and it's frustrating. The things they are doing to public health are going to cause terrible damage to the people of the country. Sometimes I want to scream, 'let me work if you're going to pay me!'"

Under the new regime, however, that wasn't possible. With the publication of a Reduction-In-Force order for the CDC in early April, the entire Office of Smoking and Health had been eliminated. When, at the end of that month, she was finally able to access her work email again, she found a RIF notice telling her that she was being terminated as of April 1. By her reckoning that meant she had been fired from a job she had already been fired from. "I've been double-dipped," she said, laughing. "But I'm still being paid."

* * *

Adrian M was having much the same experience. She, too, had been put into limbo, on indefinite Administrative Leave after the court ruling that the way the probationary workers had been fired was likely illegal; and she had likewise probably received a RIF notice that, it seemed, superseded the original reason for booting her out of government employment — though she wasn't one hundred percent sure about that, since she couldn't access her government email to find out. She, too, was realizing the likelihood that she wouldn't be brought back to work at the CDC, and was also looking, so far without success, for new employment. By late April, she estimated that she had applied for over a hundred jobs; a handful had bothered to reach out to her to tell her she hadn't gotten an interview; from the rest, there had just been silence. By mid-May, that number had ballooned to closer to 150 applications. She would put on audio books or gospel music, and would set to work tweaking her résumé to better match each job description. But none of it had borne fruit. Adrian was applying for jobs, all around the country, in both the private sector and in public health departments at a state and local level — but many of those jobs were being pulled in the wake of federal cuts to state and local grants; and the remaining ones were so inundated with applicants that oftentimes the online systems went down and couldn't accept additional applications. On one particularly frustrating occasion, she filled in all the forms, uploaded all the documents she had to upload, and then went to her kitchen to get some food. When she returned to press the "submit" button, she found the website's portal had been replaced with a 404 error message. Her assumption was that while she was preparing a snack it had maxed out on the number of applications it could receive.

None of this was helping with her anxiety. When her grandfather had died, at the age of 95, the previous year, the doctor had prescribed her with anti-anxiety medications. Now, she found that she needed to take the pills on a regular basis. She couldn't stop thinking about how vulnerable she was financially, a single woman without a partner to help her pay her bills, without someone whose health benefits she could access if and when she was finally fired. She obsessed about her friend, with metastatic ovarian cancer, and how in cutting off funding for an array of cancer research the NIH was making it more likely that her friend would die. She couldn't stop fixating on the fact that so many of the CDC's public education programs were being cut that when patients came back home from their doctor with a serious diagnosis, the government resources wouldn't be available anymore for all of the educational research that they wanted — and needed — to do to understand what challenges they were facing in the years ahead.

Most personally, Adrian M worried that, especially living in a red state, she was particularly vulnerable to a growing groundswell of racial hatred — and, indeed, she had recently experienced a deeply unpleasant, racially-tinged encounter in the crowd leaving a baseball stadium at the end of a game. Trump, she believed, was "giving permission for hate. It's open season on hate, and you can hate anyone you want to — because the Trump administration allows it." Every time another government official launched another diatribe against DEI, every time another highly qualified African American man or woman was fired from a senior position — as a general in the armed forces, as head of the Library of Congress, and so on — and replaced with a white man or woman, she felt a sense of personal betrayal. She found it hard to believe that, after all of Trump's talk about ending the hiring of unqualified people, when it came time to nominate someone for the position of Surgeon General the Administration chose a white lady with an inactive medical license.

When she drove home, north through the Carolinas and west into Tennessee, for the Easter holidays, she was disheartened to see so many Trump signs in front yards and along roadways. To stay awake, having left home at 4 a.m. to beat the holiday traffic, she sang along to Luther Vandross and Whitney Houston songs on her car music system. Her dogs, she joked, weren't amused; but it was the "little pick-me-up" that she needed. Yet, no matter how much she sang, she couldn't escape the sense of growing dread she felt. Each of the three days that she was with her family, she worried, were days that she was absent from the job hunt. What if she missed the perfect job? What if all the anti-DEI sloganeering 'morphed into something far worse — into renewed segregation, into government-licensed discrimination? Given what was happening in the country, no possibility seemed too outlandish for her.

"All the progress that has been made since the 1950s is gone," she said bitterly. Here she was, highly qualified to work in public health, and with a decade of working at the CDC on vital, life-saving, projects under her belt, and all the Trump team thought of people with her skin color was that they were part of the "waste, fraud and abuse" problem in the federal government; and that they should head off into the private sector and get some of the factory jobs that Trump was promising to bring back to America again. She viewed herself as a patriot, her work every bit as valuable to the community as the work of those who signed up to join the military, but on a daily basis she was being bombarded with public rhetoric from government officials essentially telling her that her role and that of her organization was somehow superfluous.

In her spare time, Adrian tried to calm her nerves by planting colorful canna lilies in her garden. She had taken up quilting — and mask-making — during the pandemic, and now found that sewing the intricate patterns and carefully stitching together the individual patches was profoundly therapeutic. "It's kinda like a fabric puzzle," she observed. Some of the easier quilts she could put together in a couple of weeks; but the more complex ones, such as the "vintage remix 2" that she had begun working on after being fired in February would take her months. She got tremendous satisfaction from making quilts, or bags, or other sewn items, and giving them to relatives or friends. "My love language is giving quilts to people, making things for people," she said simply. "It's definitely a good way to distract yourself."

But then she'd meet up with friends from the CDC, and all the emotions and the pain would well to the surface again. Russell Vought, she knew, had publicly stated that the aim was to traumatize federal workers so they would either resign or become ineffective. "And," said Adrian M, "that's what's happening. We are trauma-bonding. Because we are all going through it."

On Easter Sunday, Natasha Miles took a long walk with Mia along the Boulder Creek, through the park on the edge of town and then up into the canyons on the edge of the Rockies. It had snowed heavily just two days earlier, and even though the weather had rapidly warmed afterwards and the sun was now shining brightly, there were still piles of snow in the shaded areas along the waterway. Miles was dressed for the part, in a thick blue puffer jacket, and blue aviator sunglasses, in tight jeans, and gray suede boots. Her hair, slightly scraggly, was shoulder-length. Mia was pulling at her leash, delighted to be walking along the waterway.

The past two months hadn't been easy. In mid-March, as a result of the court rulings, Miles had been rehired, but had then been immediately placed on Administrative Leave. Adding insult to injury, the government hadn't sent her the paperwork to allow her to keep her health insurance active. She had told her insurance company that she'd been restored to her job, but despite her calling every day, the company wouldn't confirm that she was now covered and wouldn't cover prescriptions sent to her pharmacist.

Seemingly by the hour Miles was getting more anxious about the fact that she couldn't fill her Humira prescription and that her Crohn's disease might, as a result, flare up at any moment. Some nights, she couldn't sleep, her health worries ricocheting around her brain for hours on end. She had looked up how much Humira would cost her out of pocket; and she had found that even with a Good Rx discount, she was still looking at $2,200 a month. That would have taken a huge chunk out of the money that she was saving for retirement. In March and in early April, she had tried to stretch her remaining medications out, by taking half doses instead. But now she was running out even of those smaller doses. What made the situation worse was that she had found out, belatedly, that when the government fires a staffer, the health insurance is supposed to last another thirty days — but no-one in government had bothered to tell her this, and as a new employee she didn't know, although they had, she subsequently realized, deducted her premiums from her March and April paychecks; what's more, in the rush to fire as many people as possible, no-one had provided the necessary paperwork to the insurance company. Nor, when they rehired her, had they notified the insurer.

By now, it was academic anyways. Barely three weeks after Miles had been re-hired, she was fired again, RIF'ed out of her job by an Administration determined, at all cost, to eviscerate large parts of the federal civil service. Now, she was trying to fill in all the paperwork to get onto her husband's health insurance plan tied to his job in Illinois; but, again, the government wasn't making it easy. They hadn't provided her the formal paperwork, beyond the initial emails, confirming she had been fired that would have served as reason for her to be able to enroll in her husband's plan outside the normal enrollment period. Miles was a super-educated, super-articulate scientist, but even with all her qualifications she was struggling to navigate this healthcare morass. "My life's kind of on hold," she reported, "trying to figure all these things out."

She made an effort to keep herself busy. Reading as many scientific papers as possible. Volunteering to help train younger scientists at Penn State to do the sort of measurements she had been doing. She walked every day in the mountains and in the city's parks, looking at the open skies and the soaring mountains that she had grown to love. Some days, she drove 25 minutes along red dirt roads through the forest — and, she noted happily, past a trailhead onto the gatepost of which someone had pasted a sign "Federal Employees Make America Great" — to get to the little hamlet of Nederland, where she would do her laundry and stock up on food at B & F Mountain Market. For a treat, she would stop for a coffee at the cutesy little café, in the center of Nederland, carved out of an old wooden railway carriage. And a couple times a week she would meet up with friends from NOAA and go out for dinner either to an Indian or Italian restaurant on Boulder's north side. They would talk about their futures: should she, she wondered, try to go back to Penn State? Or should she look to find work as a contractor? Or should she take her expertise overseas — universities in France had recently opened up a number of positions for scientists looking to leave Trump's America, and she was thinking about applying?

What astounded Miles was that, even as climate change accelerated, and the window to keep the world from heating by more than the 1.5 degrees that the vast majority of scientists in her field believed represented a dangerous tipping point started to close, American government institutions and scientists would now be absented from the vital work that needed to be done.

Worse, vast amounts of climate change-related data that they had already painstakingly accumulated was being scrubbed, at speed, from government websites and databases, leaving it to non-profits, media centers, libraries, and universities to scramble to try to download the data and save it before it was permanently removed. Within ten days of Trump's inauguration, three thousand datasets had been removed from government websites. As the months rolled on, thousands upon thousands of additional web pages of government information were removed, on everything from the January 6, 2021, insurrection to climate change. *New York Times* journalist Tiffany Hsu pungently noted that "the campaign of deletion does more than amplify the administration's policy priorities — it buries evidence of the alternatives in a MAGA-branded memory hole."

The White House's Covid information page was replaced by a splashy report titled "Lab Leak" that purported to prove the pandemic was caused by a leak from a Chinese facility. In between the words "lab" and "leak" was an image of a determined Donald J. Trump, striding toward the viewer. Web pages that previously had included words such as "women" and "Black", "inequality" and "climate change" were scrubbed of the offending language. Park Service sites providing information on slavery toned down their discussions of what slavery had involved. References to African American military heroes were removed from Defense Department sites. By the summer, the Administration would be ordering Smithsonian Institution museums to adjust their exhibits to meet the new ideological standards.

Add it all up, and the destruction of this trove of knowledge wasn't all that different from the public book-burning episodes orchestrated by previous totalitarian regimes elsewhere in the world. It was about imposing a particular version of history, a particular understanding of science, and a particular narrative around race relations and immigration and gender norms.

Every so often Miles made the mistake of going on random excursions into the back alleys of social media sites, where she found, to her horror, that a shocking number of Americans were cheering on the attacks on government institutions and whooping with delight at the treatment of the public workers who were being fired. She wondered what had happened to their sense of empathy and hoped against hope that at some point they would realize just how much society lost when an agency such as NOAA was deliberately hamstrung.

For two months now, Charlie Wright had been getting up before the sun, driving out to the local rec center pool, meeting up with a few buddies, and swimming as hard and as fast as he could for sixty minutes. He loved seeing the moon still high in the sky as he went along the quiet streets. At the pool, Wright was, he acknowledged, the slowest guy in his group; but he didn't care. Every single stroke was an exercise in something approaching redemptive suffering. "I've never seen a clock move so slow," he laughed. "Every stroke, I see it and I'm like 'darn it, I swear the clock is going backwards.'" By 7:15 a.m., with the sun just beginning to rise, he was done, the intense exercise having cut the edge of his anxiety, would dress for the day — his taste ran casual: Sandals, jeans, short sleeved shirts — and head out to one of his favorite cafes for a quick coffee.

Wright had also started running again, and, when he had time, he would meditate. Anything, he figured, to remove the jitters from his day.

After weeks of constant, sleepless, anxiety, during which his mind was so agitated that he even had to take time off from coaching his kids' soccer team, recently Wright's fortunes had taken a turn for the better; a local university, some of whose scientists had previously collaborated with him on his NOAA work, offered him a temporary position, paid by the hour, and even though that meant he was earning about half what he had in his federal work he had leapt at the opportunity. After all the enforced idleness from earlier in the year, it felt great to be back in the saddle.

There had been times in the previous months when the rage he felt at how he had been treated threatened to swamp him. He couldn't fathom the cruelty of firing people, rehiring them, and then — having dangled out that glimmer of hope — re-firing them all over again. He had gone on political protests to express his anger, one of millions of people taking to the streets in cities around the country as the scale of the attacks on the federal government, and, more generally, on the rule of law became apparent. At these protests one could see everything from posters bearing pictures of Kilmar Abrego Garcia — the Salvadoran man deported to the CECOT supermax prison in El Salvador, despite a judge's explicit order to not return him to that country — through to placards critiquing the escalating corruption of the Administration. There were banners denouncing Trump's end run around Congress and his assumption of king-like powers, and other banners denouncing the fascist affiliations of many of Trump's inner circle. Wright had wanted to shout from the rooftops about the injustice of it all. But now, even though he still hadn't received the formal termination paperwork from his job and thus didn't know what benefits the government was saying he was or wasn't entitled to, he was starting to feel almost Zen about the situation. "Time cures everything. I'm at peace with it," he said, taking a sip from his coffee mug. "I'm still affected by it, but honestly I have to move on. This is an opportunity to pivot and do something different. I'm like, 'ok, there's something else out there for me!' That's the mindset I have. I'm not going back."

Wright would get into the office before eight most days, and would work well into the evening. He was throwing himself heart and soul into his new projects to distract himself from what had recently transpired in his life. For the first time since mid-February, he could see a light at the end of the tunnel. "We're all going to survive, I think," he said cautiously. "But a lot of people are hurting."

After they were fired, 24-year-old Carmen Drier planned out a road trip back East. They felt that they were young enough to start again — that they would, indeed, survive, without too much damage having been done, and the plan was to spend some time at the parental home in New Jersey before working out next steps. But then, as the court cases progressed, it began to look more likely that their job would be restored.

Drier recalibrated. They had planned to leave on a Sunday; but the Wednesday before, they received a call from their boss saying that the rehiring process would begin soon. Instead of heading back east, Drier quickly mapped out a swing through California instead. The redwoods of Sequioa, then south and west to Santa Barbara, to take in the stunning coast and the Spanish colonial-style downtown. Visit some cousins in Los Angeles then over to Redlands where they had friends from an earlier internship. Down to San Diego for some hiking in Torrey Pines and along the Sunset Cliffs above the Pacific Ocean. Out to Poway, where their dad had grown up. And finally back northeast, to Death Valley.

They had always wanted to visit Death Valley, to hike the canyons and walk atop the sand dunes, to look up, at night, at one of the best skies on earth. It met expectations. One night, they made friends with Park Rangers at a star-gazing event, bonding over the chaos that had been unleashed in the federal government — weeks later Trump would unveil a budget proposal that included a nearly one billion dollar cut to the National Park Service, as well as announcing a plan to return some of the smaller national parks to state park status, signaling a remarkable departure from Teddy Roosevelt's vision of an expansive national park system to protect the country's most spectacular and important landscapes. They slept in their car, with heat insulation foil in the windows — it was that in-between time when the valley could still be bone-chillingly cold at night, and, once the sun came up, rapidly become a furnace — a couple miles outside of the Stovepipe Wells campground.

And then, having at least partially scratched their Death Valley itch, they pointed their car north again, and headed back to a job that, unlike those of so many others who had been dumped into Administrative Leave limbo, seemed to actually be a real, in-person, 9-to-5 affair. "Man, what a weird feeling," they laughed. "It's been exciting to come back. When I came back, people gave me lots of hugs and a welcome back balloon and Hershey's kisses." But they couldn't shake the feeling that none of it was real, that they were in some ways a ghost brought back to haunt their previous workplace. At times, they wondered what it would be like to pack it all in and look for work in a place with less drama and less of an uncertain outlook. But then their inner voice told them there was still a story to be told at the US Geological Survey. Moreover, they didn't want to give the people who had tried to fire them the sense of success that would come with their quitting. "I like my fricking job," they exclaimed. "And I think it's important. And it's wrong what happened."

But Drier recognized the deck was stacked against them. "Everyone's just stressed out beyond belief, and it's really not good." Reading the writing on the wall, many USGS scientists and other staff were taking the pay-outs that were still being offered, in the process removing with them accumulated generations of scientific knowledge and skills. "It's not pleasant, really. No, it's not great. People are having non-stop meetings about different data culls; people are quitting. How do we recover from this?" So many people had left by mid-April that it was becoming all-but impossible to complete existing projects, let alone to plant the seeds for new ones. Mordantly, one of Drier's co-workers had put up a board in his office on which he had written the names of all the scientists at the center and the number of years they had worked for the USGS. Many of them, Drier realized one day, had been there for longer than she had been alive. Each day, as more left, the colleague crossed their names off of the list. By late April, somewhere in the region of a quarter of the USGS employees at the office had quit.

Others were, for the moment, sticking it out. But even they were obsessively scrolling Reddit feeds looking for the latest information from workers at other agencies on impending DOGE cuts and RIFs, trying to read the tea leaves for what was coming their way. For Drier it kind of made sense. "A lot of these people are scientists. So that's how they cope — trying to find definitive answers."

As for the fresh-out-of-college Drier, they were just waiting for the axe to fall. In late April, Human Resources had sent out an email saying they were collecting data on employees for the RIF. Ostensibly, this was so that survivors of the upcoming purge could be moved around to plug the gaps created by mass firings. Drier suspected it was just a way to grease all of their departures.

Meanwhile, each week they were still getting DOGE emails demanding all the employees list the five things they had done to justify their continued employment. It had become a cat-and-mouse game: the emails would come in, and, *en masse*, the employees would report them to human resources as suspected phishing. Recently, however, that option had been curtailed. On April 22, the Department of Interior's DC office — which had already raised Drier's hackles by making them attend long presentations on how AI would make the department more efficient and how the United States would once again become energy dominant — had sent out an email saying that the "phishing button" via which they could report a suspect email had been permanently removed from the Outlook email system.

For all of the at-risk federal employees, official emails seemed only to signify bad news. Hannah Echt opened her email just before the end of business on Friday, May 2. In her inbox was a note sent, at 3:51 p.m., to all of the AFGE union local members in NIOSH. "Happy Friday AFGE 3840," the email began. "Please see the attached union notification." When the members clicked on the notification, each found that they had received a personalized RIF notice. "Dear HANNAH ECHT," Echt's one stated. "I regret to inform you that you are being affected by a reduction in force (RIF) action. ... This RIF action does not reflect directly on your service, performance, or conduct. It is being taken solely for reasons stated in the memorandum."

Bizarrely, the email went on to inform her that she would lose her access to the building she worked in starting April 1 — more than a month before the letter was emailed out, but the date that all the supervisors in the office had been fired during the preliminary implementation of the reduction-in-force; and it then helpfully advised her to save this email for her records, or to forward it to her personal email address. She would, a follow-up email sent later that night said, be kept on staff until July 2, but only in an Administrative Leave capacity — paid to do nothing as workplace safety issues multiplied — and then she would officially be "separated" from the agency she had worked at.

The initial Health and Human Services email ended, disingenuously, "Leadership at HHS appreciates your service." Given the way that she and her organization had been treated, and given the Trump administration's determination to immediately shut down, or hobble, not only NIOSH but also multiple other workplace safety and regulatory agencies, as well as agencies such as the Consumer Financial Protection Bureau that protected consumers of financial services from predatory and dishonest lending practices, that didn't exactly seem accurate. It might well have been more honest for the author to have written "Leadership at HHS really doesn't care at all for your service, and, in keeping with the priorities of the new oligarchy, we don't actually see the point in the lifesaving work you have done over the years."

Even though Echt knew that at some point she would get such an email, it still knocked her off-kilter. "Friday night," she mused regarding the timing. "That kind of ruins the weekend." She went home stunned, emotionally drained, and spent the next couple of days curled up with her cats and binge-reading Hilary Mantel's historic fiction trilogy on Henry VIII and his Machiavellian chief advisor, Thomas Cromwell, as well as a weighty history of the Byzantine empire.

On Monday, Echt and her colleagues were back in the office, clearing out their boxes of notes, their books, their half-finished worksite evaluations, the degree certificates that they had hung from their walls, and their other personal effects. It was, Echt, who had always craved order and predictability, felt, "very upsetting. I really didn't want to pack up my stuff." She felt stressed, felt like things were happening that she couldn't control, felt that her most basic daily routines had been upended. But pack it up she did, thankful, at the end of the day, that, unlike her colleagues with twenty-plus years of work files to sort through, she could do the whole thing in barely an hour. When she had finished piling the boxes into her car, she joined some of her colleagues in the office cafeteria. They were planning a rally outside of their HHS building that evening, after the end of the workday, and needed to make signs. Echt made hers out of foamboard. It showed a tombstone, with the words "RIP: Health Hazard Evaluations, 1970-2025."

At 5 p.m. dozens of them headed out to the sidewalk to protest the assault on NIOSH. They were joined by onlookers who also wanted to express their anger at what was happening. As cars drove past, the drivers honked in support. It wasn't much, but to the protestors it was at least a straw that they could grasp at. Echt stood up and gave a brief, impassioned, speech about how far they had come in building public support for their campaign to save their workplace. None of this would, she knew, change things overnight, but the young industrial hygienist kept hoping against hope that eventually all of the protesting, the lobbying, the publicity would pay off. She took heart from the fact that, over the past few days, HHS had begun issuing public denials that NIOSH was being killed, saying it was simply a restructuring, that basic functions would continue, and that employees weren't being terminated. These claims were, as all of the RIF'ed workers knew, bald-faced lies, but at least, Echt figured, it meant that someone in HHS had realized they were starting to get slammed by bad publicity.

As her last day at NIOSH wound down, Hannah Echt and her colleagues packed up their signs and headed over to a local brewery, for what she joked would be a most "un-Happy Hour." There, over pints of lager, they discussed the rally and their future plans. How best to keep the spotlight on NIOSH, how to fight back against the cuts. Many of them had played together on the office softball team — Echt was a catcher, and had scored a run the first game of the season — and now they wondered if they would be able to continue with the team even though they no longer had a workplace at which to anchor it.

They would be going to Washington, DC two weeks later, riding busses chartered by the union, to meet with legislators and to pitch them on the importance of saving NIOSH. On the 22nd, they, along with fellow union members from the NIOSH offices in Pittsburgh and Morgantown, would be holding a demonstration outside of the HHS headquarters. Echt was, in a strange way, excited about it; she had only been to the nation's capital once before, on a school band trip when she was in eighth grade. But, at the same time, she was struck by how bizarre it was to have to be traveling the country by bus in order to lobby to keep on doing the work that she loved. "I'd rather be doing my actual job than my new job — which is trying to save my actual job!" she exclaimed, laughing.

Daniel Dodd-Ramirez and his colleagues at the Consumer Financial Protection Bureau were growing increasingly cynical about the way the government was functioning. For months now, they hadn't been allowed to do any work, and paranoia was running high on their Signal chats. Each and every rumor of them being imminently RIF'ed circulated and recirculated again — and, with the human resources department having also been put into deep freeze, there was no-one left to go to so as to inquire regarding the veracity of the rumors; Dodd-Ramirez was convinced that, if the RIF notices came in, as a 55-year-old he would be forcibly sent into early retirement. People had started moving into other rooms from their computers when they talked on Signal, wary lest their laptops had been compromised by the government or by DOGE and converted into spy tools against the beleaguered agency's staff. "It's really something!" Daniel Dodd-Ramirez said in amazement, as he pondered how his own colleagues were behaving as did dissidents in the ex-Soviet Union and other totalitarian systems. "We're not involved in national security for Chrissake. We're not military or intelligence. It's just the way we've been treated." That anxiety was hardly alleviated by reports of government officials in some agencies being made to take lie detector tests in an effort to ferret out whistleblowers, by criminal investigations launched against high profile one-time government officials, and by reports that investigators were being hired specifically to go after public sector workers in USAID and other gutted agencies who had had the temerity to talk about their situation to the press.

"Everybody's waiting," Dodd-Ramirez observed. Would the courts let the Administration reduce the Consumer Financial Protection Bureau's staff from about 1,500 to a mere 100? The bureau had been established by Congress, and the Dodd-Frank Act mandated it do certain functions that, he explained, couldn't possibly be carried out by a skeleton staff. When government lawyers testified before Congress that reducing the staff levels by more than 90 percent would still leave the CFPB in compliance with the Dodd-Frank Act, and when they claimed that the bureau's workforce was getting on with work as normal, Dodd-Ramirez was incredulous. It was, he fumed, the biggest example of gaslighting that he'd ever seen. "Nobody's asking us to work. They are making pretenses, but they aren't allowing us into work; they have no interest in knowing the work that we do, or in sharing their priorities for us. Their interest is dismantling the agency." For a while his unit tried to keep up the charade, holding noon virtual work meetings every Tuesday on Teams. But after a while those became little more than group therapy sessions, where people discussed which anti-depressants their doctors had put them on, and then they dwindled and stopped altogether — after all, there was no ongoing bureau work to talk about.

Knowing their days at the bureau were numbered, and depressed as a result of not being allowed into the office they had worked in for years, many of Dodd-Ramirez's colleagues were trying to get ahead of the curve, looking for work all over the country.

And yet, they had found only slim pickings. Highly trained in consumer advocacy work, in financial investigations, in litigation, they nevertheless found the job market a turbulent one to navigate. Dodd-Ramirez himself had also begun the job search and had also so far drawn blanks — moreover, he had concluded that even should a job land in his lap, it would likely pay far less than what he was earning at the CFPB. In consequence, he and his wife were thinking of renting out rooms in their Roanoke, Virginia home, which they had only recently moved into after deciding to leave DC, to cover their bills should he be RIF'ed.

While they waited, many volunteered, for food banks and for humane societies. After all, these were men and women who had spent careers advocating for the poor and the exploited. Now they were watching the US government take the axe to social safety net programs from the Low Income Heating and Energy Assistance Program [LIHEAP], which helped 6.7 million families with their heating and energy bills through to Medicaid and Food Stamps — both of which stood to have to absorb swingeing cuts as the GOP outlined its budget priorities for the coming years. Previously, the CFPB had had a focus on helping immigrants; now, the federal apparatus was being marshalled *against* immigrants, with some particularly unfortunate migrants being shipped off either to Guantanamo Bay or to El Salvador's ghastly CECOT supermax prison. "The fear creeps in," Dodd-Ramirez admitted. "Your mind can go to some dark places when you're going through what we're going through. A lot of people are going through a lot of depression, fear, sadness, and even suicidal ideation."

Faced with the administration's governing priorities, and its distaste for helping the poor or the weak, it was small wonder that so many of the CFPB crew decided to turn to charity work to at least partially assuage the damage being done by the roll-back of federal government functions and obligations. Dodd-Ramirez put in the hours advising the staff of his meditation center in Georgia and began sketching out a way to start, and secure funding for, a nonprofit that would help consumers, in a miniaturized version of the bureau he was now parting ways from; he hoped to take four of five of his colleagues with him. Some of the put-out-to-grass employees spent more time with their pets — one of his female colleagues had two lizards, oth-ers had more run-of-the-mill cats and dogs. Some colleagues had taken up gardening with a passion; others baking. One was even thinking of packing in the whole help-the-consumer gig and starting his own business.

All Dodd-Ramirez knew was that he was damn proud of the work he had done. There were poor people who were just slightly less poor as a result of the CFPB's actions. There were cut-throat financial companies that were just a tad more respectful of the consumers who accessed their products as a result of the pres-sure of CFPB lawsuits.

Some days, it seemed, Kelsey Hendrix was starting to forget how to laugh. The past few months had been a nonstop rollercoaster.

Like thousands of other federal workers, she had been fired in the initial wave of purges and then had been called back to her job once some of the court cases brought against the firings began bearing fruit, with judges issuing preliminary injunctions against the Administration. Unlike many of them, however, she hadn't accepted a deferred resignation offer in those first days back, and now, on April 10 that decision had come back to haunt her. A federal appeals court had ruled that, in the case of NOAA, pending resolution of the case the agency didn't have to keep its probationary workers on the payroll.

Hendrix's termination notice had come through at 5:30 p.m. on Thursday, April 10, and it was backdated to declare that her actual termination date was February 27. In an act of faux-generosity, Hendrix and the other re-fired employees were told that they wouldn't have to reimburse the federal government for the back-pay they had received for the intervening five weeks. She laughed, bitterly, at the thought that they would have even considered making the employees give back that income.

Truth be told, Hendrix had been expecting to be re-fired. It was clear to her the Administration would move hell and high water to not be stuck with these employees for the duration. But it still stung, still felt terribly bleak. She was tired, numb. She felt that with all the chaos inflicted on the federal workers she hadn't had time to breathe properly in months. She felt like she was a pinball ricocheting around a machine that she had no control over. She worried about her arthritis flaring up, as she hadn't managed to fill her prescriptions for the extremely expensive medication that she was on since she had first been fired and was thus still relying on ibuprofen to dull the pain. Soon, she knew, without the medications that she needed, "things would go completely sideways." And she worried about how to access insurance down the line, since the Office of Personnel Management *still* hadn't sent her — or her colleagues — any of the paperwork needed to access continued insurance once she had been separated from NOAA. She was, finally, resigned to the fact that she would have to apply for Medicaid, which meant that she would have to spend down her savings. And she had started cutting basic items out of her household budget. Did she and her boyfriend *really* need Netflix, or could they scrap that monthly expense? Those were the sorts of questions she was now asking herself.

"I have to be optimistic, because if not then we're in trouble," she declared. "I hope I can get a new job, but I don't know. There are so many people looking for jobs right now. And if more people get fired, it will only get harder." Pretty much every ex-federal employee she knew who had managed to get a new job had had to take a massive pay cut. It was ironic, she noted, since many of these men and women had left lucrative private sector jobs and taken reduced pay because they wanted to work in the public sector and make a difference. Now, they were being fired from that public sector, entering a job market entirely saturated with other desperate people who had lost their federal employment, and taking a second pay cut simply to purchase some footing in the rat race again.

"It's been an interesting time," was how she put it. "I feel for the HR people stuck processing our paperwork over and over and over again." Part of her held out hope that the lawsuit filed by Democratic state Attorneys General against the indiscriminate cuts would pay off; another part of her hoped the case the unions had brought would, on appeal, result in a victory for the workers. But, deep down, she was already starting to disengage from the public sector. She had begun applying for procurement-type jobs with private companies, as well as for customer service gigs, work that came with a starting salary about thirty thousand dollars a year less than what she had been making at NOAA. That, however, wasn't the only obstacle. When she applied for jobs, she was confronted with a quandary: On the application forms, it asked her if she had ever been fired — and, because of the way the government had treated her, the only answer she could give was "yes."

In mid-April, Taly Lind flew out to New York to see her daughter performing in an Off-Broadway musical.

Since she had been placed on Administrative Leave, Lind had been going through what she freely admitted was a roller-coaster of emotions. Some days, such as when she was studying to become a birth and post-partum doula — a non-medically trained person who helps women navigate birth and the weeks and months following — she felt like she could take on anything and anyone. When she received word that she had gotten into a master's program in social work at George Mason University — the classes of which she could take remotely, followed by a couple of years of part-time, unpaid, work experience — she was on top of the world. It had, after all, always been a dream of hers to one day do social work with at-risk youth. Other days, though, she couldn't contain her anger and her sorrow. She would watch a particularly upsetting news report on TV, about, say, the ongoing crisis in Gaza, and, realizing USAID no longer existed to even *try* to mitigate the worst of the crisis, suddenly burst into tears. Her husband told her that her ability to control her anger seemed to have waned; she had to admit there was truth to the charge.

Many nights, Taly Lind found herself wide awake at three o'clock. Again and again she would think of the kids overseas dying of starvation because they were no longer receiving

30-cent bags of Plumpy'Nut paste. She repeatedly checked to see whether the situation had been resolved and whether permission had been granted to ship the supplies from US warehouses to distributors overseas. As of late April, that permission still had not been issued. She would start doom-scrolling on her phone, second-guessing how disasters would have been responded to had USAID still been on the ground. Other sleepless nights, taking advantage of the different time zones, she would phone or text friends in various states in the US and overseas.

The journey east to New York was a long one — ten hours if one flew from Honolulu direct, more if, like the soon-to-be-ex-federal-worker, one opted for the less expensive route, which involved a change of planes in Atlanta. Lind donned a USAID sweatshirt for the flights, and packed a USAID tote bag, as well as a beige USAID T shirt, adorned with Trump's description of USAID workers as being "radical lunatics." If the agency that she loved was to be destroyed, at least she could, in the months leading up to the date of her termination, become a walking advertisement for it. There was a bitter irony to all the publicity around the DOGE cuts; in the past, she had found that almost no-one knew what USAID was, or what it did. Now, with the agency having been destroyed, strangers would see her shirt or her bag and offer her their condolences for what had happened. Even her hairdresser, in Honolulu, was aware of what had gone down.

Lind spent a little over a week in the Big Apple, staying with her in-laws on the Upper West Side and visiting with her daughter. What a "nachus," a joy, it was, she said in Yiddish, to see her daughter thriving, doing exactly what she wanted to be doing, and on a stage in New York no less. "I can't even tell you what that feels like," she enthused. "You can't beat that." She was as excited about being in New York to see her daughter on stage as she was about the family's upcoming trip, in mid-May, to Japan — a trip that she and her husband had sprung for, almost against their better judgement, for themselves, their two kids and their kids' partners, to celebrate their son's upcoming graduation from university.

From New York, Lind took the Amtrak train south to DC, where she would spend the next week couch-surfing at friends' houses.

There were two events drawing Taly Lind to the Capital: The first was a "bring your kids to work day," which — since the USAID workers no longer had an office to bring their children to — many of Lind's erstwhile colleagues had decided to turn into an impromptu lobbying effort. Those with young children, as well as those, like Lind, without — both her daughter, in New York, and her son, studying at University of Massachusetts, Amherst, had long flown the roost — decided to show up at their Congressional representatives' offices to put in their two cents-worth about the importance of overseas aid work. Those with kids had gotten the children to write letters, explaining to the members of the House and Senate exactly how proud they were to have parents who had done good work overseas, and how sad they were that their parents could no longer do that work.

One eight-year-old girl wrote that "I learned about USAID when my mom worked with them for many years and I think it is really important. USAID is like a kind helper from America. They go to other countries to help people who need it. If someone is hungry, they bring food. If kids need a school, they help build one. If someone is sick, they help doctors take care of them... I think USAID is like a superhero team that helps people around the world live better lives." Another girl wrote, "I am eight years old and even i know that USAID is important. My mom and my dad work for USAID but are getting fired. My dad helps families be resilient and my mom helps people get food." A fifth grader wrote to their senator, "with USAID getting closed down, many people from around the world might suffer from all sorts of terrible things, including poverty... We need your help to put a stop to this nonsense."

Lind met up with representatives from Senator Gillibrand's office — since she and her husband thought it likely they would soon move back to New York; her colleagues met up with other politicians who had previously expressed support for USAID. These were mainly Democrats, but did include a handful of Republican senators, including ex-majority leader Mitch McConnell.

The lobbying effort was important, but perhaps the bigger DC draw for Lind was a picnic, scheduled to start at noon on April 25, that she had put heart and soul into organizing. It would bring about a hundred of her USAID colleagues onto the Jefferson Pier Stone area, due west of the Washington Monument, in the center of the Mall, to chew over old times and mourn their new circumstances. Lind and others had worked the Signal chats getting people to commit to attending. It would be, she felt, a way to reaffirm the power of their community, something of a catharsis, even, for people who had had the rug pulled out from under them. After all, she noted, if you're in the foreign service you live your lives overseas, "away from family, away from people we've grown up with." Instead, you substitute in the camaraderie of co-workers, people who, like you, are devoted to a cause and throw heart and soul into a project. And then, suddenly, with a few tweets and a few well-placed DOGE gut-punches, it all comes to a screeching halt, and you're scattered to the winds.

Lind and her colleagues, many of them wearing some form or other of USAID swag — Lind, with her frizzy shoulder length hair blowing in the breeze, wore her beige "radical lunatic" T-shirt, brown slacks, and rainbow-patterned ankle socks — turned up to the Jefferson Pier Stone with their picnic boxes laden down with food. To make things simple, the organizer had suggested they each just bring their own lunches. Of course, that wasn't what happened. Each person came with food to share, meaning that, as they sat on the grass under a lightly clouded sky, the early spring weather warm enough for some of them to be wearing shorts, they had far more to eat than was needed. But that, Lind realized, was a perfect outcome for a USAID gathering. "That is us in a nutshell," she said. "We're all about feeding people."

Over the course of five hours, the picnickers shared stories. One woman had applied for 214 jobs since she had received her termination notice, but so far hadn't landed new work. Another explained how she had been advised, on the QT, to tone down her USAID employment history, since in the new Trump era such a work history was viewed by potential employers as "toxic." Lind herself talked about how she, too, had been applying for jobs, at nonprofits, and at NGOs, even with overseas government aid organizations, but so far hadn't managed to get an interview.

As the July 2 date of her termination crept closer, Taly Lind was feeling increasingly outraged about how she and her fellow workers had been treated. She felt that there was nothing more patriotic than doing the soft-power work they had done at USAID, and "nothing more American than wanting to show the best of America to the rest of the world." No matter how many different ways she tried to look at it, she couldn't see any justification for tearing down the entire foreign aid edifice.

From his basement windows, high up on the walls, Dan Meleason could just about see the Rockies. He would sit there, most afternoons, at the large red oak table that he had made back when he was living in DC — a table that, in happier times, he and his partner and their friends would do large jigsaw puzzles on — scrolling through job listings on his laptop. It had been something of a dispiriting search. True, there were jobs out there, but there was also a surfeit of newly unemployed skilled workers seeking to fill those positions. Ideally, he said, sardonically, he wanted a job "by last week;" realistically, he was hoping to find something by September. Meleason was looking all over the country — had even started exploring options in western Canada. And he and his partner were openly discussing the idea of going further afield still, to Australia or New Zealand, maybe, or somewhere in Europe. To that end, he had begun taking Duolingo courses in French and was enrolled in some online language classes via his local public library.

Every so often, the ex-cryptologist would realize that his mind had wandered away from the task at hand and that he was catastrophizing, gaming out in his mind what would happen during fire season given the numbers of Forest Service employees the USDA had terminated. "There's going to be a lot of people burnt out," he feared. "There will probably be pretty catastrophic losses — people and property. It's going to be very sad,

I think. I think it'll be pretty bad, honestly." What made him want to tear his hair out was that people were still approaching this as a Red/Blue issue — with the Blues favoring government employees and the Reds wanting to eviscerate the public sector wherever and however they could. It made no sense to Meleason. "Flora doesn't care where the policy lines are drawn, he said," explaining that flammable vegetation could crop up anywhere. "And fire certainly doesn't."

Meleason wasn't sleeping well. Just as had happened during Trump 1.0, he was having nightmares, oftentimes involving real-life meetings he had been in with senior government officials in which he'd warned of what would happen if Trump's team did or didn't do something the consequences of which would be particularly jarring to the international order. For the first time since 2021, he was back on the pills he had been prescribed, medications given to veterans suffering from PTSD, that helped him to go to sleep and to stay asleep through the night. An old tug of depression was back, threatening to plunge him into a dark place he would far rather not go. He seemed to be perennially anxious, worried that at any moment his Administrative Leave would be ended and he would formally be fired. He worried that he would have to pay back to the federal government the back pay he had received after being reinstated. Whenever an email from someone in USDA popped up in his inbox, he could feel himself recoil in alarm. Recently, he had felt the emails were almost exercises in trolling. Basically, they told him he was still employed but only because a federal judge had put a hold on the firing of probationary employees — and that the USDA was actively fighting the ruling. In essence, he felt, they were warning him, "don't get too comfortable; we're still coming after you."

Mornings, he would attempt to shake the night jitters by going on long walks with his dogs in city parks, hoping that the beauty of nature would help him reset his brain. He would take his mountain bike up into the hills. Some days, he would organize rock climbing adventures on the fifty feet walls along Shelf Road with old friends. Meleason found it almost meditative and wanted to do more of this as the weather warmed. There was something intoxicating in the combination of emotions it conjured up; there was the fear of falling and of the unknown — but there was also the sense of calm one got when having to focus all of one's energies on finding the next hand and foot placement, on shifting the distribution of weights to secure a hold, of trying to precisely pivot one's body over to the next safe spot. "You really don't think about too much else," he said. "The latest tweet, or what stupid decisions are being made in DC."

Meleason was up for trying pretty much anything if it would offer a distraction from the political chaos, something that would stop him feeling like he was sitting on pins and needles. He didn't like the sensation of always wondering, "What's going to be next?" He and his partner had begun going to bowling alleys with their neighbors. He was reading voraciously — Walter Isaacson's book *Codebreaker*, on the discoverers of CRISPR; William Finnegan's volume on surfing. He was watching a lot of comedy shows on TV. His partner and he had dived into a slew of home improvement projects, from remodeling a bathroom through to planting flowers in their garden.

Sometimes all of these diversions worked; but other times he sank lower into a pit of despair. "It's hard to reconcile my belief that wanting to work for the federal government is a privilege — you're doing things for the people of the United States; you're trying to do the right thing for everyone in the US..." He stopped, thought about it, and began again. "I've really questioned: if we're stymied by what's happening at the top of the proverbial food chain then what's the point? I question why I wanted to come back in federal service. I get kind of depressed because of that. It's not what I expected when I re-signed up to work for the people of the United States. It truly isn't."

When he tried to analyze what was going on in his head, he realized he was grieving. "I'm angry all the time, because I can see the writing on the wall; and I'm frustrated, because people are turning a blind eye to what is happening. Maybe that's the next step of grieving: the crying, the madness, and now I'm at the frustration point."

PART THREE

FUCK AROUND AND FIND OUT

When she went for her annual physical, Aryn Backus's doctor told her she remembered that Backus worked for the CDC and volunteered her observation that now must not be a great time to be in such a job. "If you ever need anti-anxiety medications, let me know!"

It was an amusing interaction, Backus felt, but there was more than a grain of truth underlying the doctor's offer. The CDC worker was seeing a therapist; but she was still having trouble sleeping, and she had developed a short fuse with her husband, snapping at him over small issues that, in the past, wouldn't have resulted in a fight. They had been planning to finish the basement in their home, so that it could serve as an office for her husband, who worked remotely. Now, worried that her Administrative Leave salary would suddenly be yanked away by one adverse court decision, they put off that home improvement. They had wanted to buy a second car; but now that was an expense that seemed to make no sense. Their dog needed surgery for urethral stones that had rendered him somewhat incontinent, but, again, that was money they didn't feel they had. Their one-year-old son was in daycare — and she was desperate to keep him in it so that she would have downtime during the day to look for new jobs — but, again, that was a significant monthly expense that was coming, increasingly, to look like a luxury they might have to do without.

Most personally hurtful of all was that they wanted to have a second child but now were desperately worried that if and when her income disappeared they wouldn't have the financial resources to support two children. "With everything going on, it's hard to make that decision, for sure," Backus said softly. She thought they still had plenty of time to expand their family — she and her husband were, after all, only in their early thirties; but, still, she worried. The financial uncertainty was, she acknowledged sadly, "a factor we have to consider."

The uncertainty was starting to gnaw at her sense of self-confidence. Every day, she woke up and felt that her life was in limbo. She was struggling to plan ahead, to imagine the future more than a few weeks or months down the line. It all felt "befuddling." It also felt horribly pre-meditated, as if powerful government officials were going out of their way to make her feel as traumatized as possible — as if they were going out of their way to make sure that federal workers such as herself never would want to work for the government again. "They took a sledgehammer to everything. They're ruining people's lives, ruining people's careers, and it doesn't make any sense to me," she stated. "They wanted to get a lot done in their first one hundred days. They're all about the numbers. And I think they really don't care about the way this is impacting everyday people."

If she sat still for too long, the anger began bubbling up anew. And so, to cut its edge, she had begun jogging again, miles each day, in training for a half marathon that she hoped to compete in later in the year. It helped, as did the yoga that she had also started practicing. But nothing could fully neutralize her growing unease.

As the summer neared, Backus couldn't stop thinking about the scale of the damage to the country's public health infrastructure that was being done. It all seemed so penny wise and pound foolish, so very shortsighted. To save a relatively small amount of federal dollars, the government was forcing out CDC workers who had decades of institutional knowledge to pass down; it was closing specialty labs that could diagnose diseases that no other labs in the country had the capacity to do; it was shutting down help lines for smokers looking for resources that would help them kick their nicotine habits; and it was erasing data that had taken years to generate. Under Robert Kennedy's leadership, the Department of Health and Human Services was also encouraging parents to doubt the safety of vaccines that had been given, to life-saving effect, to generations of children. She couldn't for the life of her see how any of this made America healthy again. Nor could she fathom how eviscerating global public health efforts was in America's national security interests — given that other countries, China chief among them, would leap at the opportunity to become globally indispensable in public health arenas that the United States was now absenting itself from.

With the summer fast approaching, Charlie Wright found himself in a strange place. Part of him had firmly moved on already; but another part of him was still seething, horrified not only at how he had been treated but at the chaos descending on the country.

Every so often Wright received, on his personal Gmail account, emails from the Department of Commerce, such as the one in early May begrudgingly acknowledging that he hadn't been fired for poor performance, as the initial termination letter had erroneously stated, but had lost his job because of a department decision to downsize the workforce. He also received periodic updates from the Office of Human Capital Services and the Office of Special Counsel about the appeals the probationary workers had filed against their dismissals. Every so often, he talked with old friends at NOAA, those who had survived the firings, had not taken the deferred resignation offers, and had not decided to call it a day and retire. They were, he said, simply buried in work, some of them trying to do the jobs that in the past two or even three workers would have filled.

Wright was happy in his new position at the university, though he knew it was only guaranteed for a few months, and his search for more permanent work had, so far, drawn only blanks. He had applied for everything from local government positions to private sector jobs, but despite his myriad qualifications, somehow employers weren't biting. He had put in applications for dozens of jobs. In some cases the rejections, based he came to think on AI filtering, would come back within minutes of his having uploaded his application. "It's damn-near impossible to get a job right now," he fumed. "Our skills from the government aren't directly translatable to the outside world." His wife had also been looking for work, but, so far, similarly without success.

In the meantime, Wright was keeping as active as possible. The last thing he wanted was to hide himself away and slide back into the sort of depression that had threatened to swamp him in the dogdays of winter in the immediate aftermath of his being fired. He had always hoped to one day learn the drums, so now he was indulging that fantasy. "I want to prove to myself that at the age of 48 I can do it," he explained. "I can get the synapses firing in different parts of my brain." He was meditating frequently; was coaching his kids' sport teams; and, perhaps most challenging, was trying to learn some Swedish on Duolingo.

It wasn't a random linguistic itch. For the past year, since well before his government job had been taken from him, he and his wife had been planning a big Scandinavian trip. Neither of their children had ever been overseas before, and, they figured, they were now old enough to get full value from a trip abroad. And so they had scrimped and saved, bought tickets from the US to Toronto, from Toronto onto Copenhagen, and then from there over to Stockholm. They were planning to tool around not just in the capital cities but also in the surrounding countryside, taking advantage of the efficient rail networks to see as much as possible in two weeks.

After Wright had lost his job, they briefly considered canceling the trip, but then they concluded it was too important, that both of them really wanted their kids to be exposed to other cultures — and that, when push came to shove, if they had to pull money out of their retirement accounts to cover the cost of the holiday, that was something they were willing to do.

Wright was paying particular attention to the news out of Scandinavia. For months, Trump had been threatening to annex the Danish territory of Greenland, either through buying it out or even through military force — an unprecedented threat given that Denmark was a NATO ally and that, since World War Two, the US had been permitted to station troops on the island. Its sea lanes, opening as the Arctic ice melted, and its large reserves of rare earth metals, uranium and other valuable assets were, Trump continually asserted, vital to US national security. "One way or another," he menacingly informed Congress, during his address to the body in February, he would make Greenland American.

As the rhetoric around Greenland had ramped up, so had the politically charged visits. The real estate tycoon's sons had made a fact-finding visit to Greenland early in the presidency, and Vice President Vance had followed up with a quick trip to the island, ostensibly to visit American forces stationed there, that had elicited formal protests from the Danish government.

Now, as the Wrights' trip neared, the newspapers were reporting that the Danes had discovered a US spying operation in Greenland and the seas beyond. Meanwhile, the Stockholm city government had recently received a letter from the US embassy in Sweden, couched in legalese, that demanded Stockholm immediately end all of its diversity, equity and inclusion policies. It was an unprecedented demand for the capital city of a sovereign nation to recalibrate its internal policies so as to align with the Trump administration's escalating assault — aimed at universities, government institutions, private companies, law offices, cultural institutions — on diversity, equity and inclusion within the US Not surprisingly, the Stockholm city council chose not to oblige the US with a positive response.

For Wright, these events represented yet more examples of the dismal turn that US politics had taken. He was more than embarrassed by what was going on. Thank goodness for the days they would spend in Toronto, on the way to Europe, he thought. They could go shopping for Canadian swag, he decided — sweatshirts, bags, T shirts, anything that could visibly indicate the family's connection to Canada. "We're going to wear them around Europe," he promised, "to let the locals know we're not obnoxious Americans." When they talked with Europeans, he pledged to himself, they would also make sure to apologize for the way the Administration was trash-talking Europe.

In the meantime, as the school year wound down and the family waited to embark on their adventure, Wright sat back and watched. On a daily basis, the scale of the federal crisis was becoming clearer. In May, the news was filled with stories about a near-catastrophe in the skies surrounding Newark airport — where an antiquated air traffic control system failed and the overworked controllers lost radar contact with all incoming aircraft for thirty seconds. In the weeks following, so many of the too few controllers left to staff the airport took time off for the mental trauma they suffered during the radar blackout that thousands of flights had to be cancelled or rerouted. Wright's wife phoned United Airlines and scrambled to reroute their flights so that they didn't have to change planes in Newark.

What was happening in Newark was, Wright thought, emblematic of a far bigger problem that the country was facing. As federal jobs were eliminated and entire agencies shuttered, vital work would simply be left undone. "We're going to lose a lot of good science," he predicted. "We're going to see a lot of research go away."

In conversations with friends and colleagues, Wright had been hearing the same colloquialism uttered again and again: "Fuck Around and Find Out — FAFO." He laughed. "We're doing that right now with these cuts — with fire season coming up, hurricane season coming up. We're screwing around and we're going to see, pretty soon, the error of our ways."

Like Charlie Wright, Taly Lind had also decided to make the best of her situation by traveling overseas with her family. In mid-May, she and her husband, her son and daughter and both of their partners, flew to Tokyo. On the flight, Lind again wore her USAID sweatshirt — earning her sympathetic words from a flight attendant furious at how DOGE had treated the agency. They would spend the next month traveling from one city to another in Japan, exploring shrines and temples, and indulging all of their love for Japanese food.

Lind had, by now, started her asynchronous courses in the remote graduate school program in social work that she had enrolled in earlier in the spring. She would get up at six am each morning and put in three hours of classwork before the family would head out on their sightseeing adventures. Late evenings, after they returned to their hotel exhausted from all the walking — her Fitbit informed her they were getting in about 25,000 steps per day — she would put in a couple additional hours on her required readings. The course was giving her at least some renewed faith in community. "I'm very excited about how much of a focus there is on human rights and social justice," she enthused. "There is a real ethical standard among social workers." They were, she felt, "people who really view the world the way I do. That's been very heartening to me."

The part-time master's program was designed to take three years, and, down the road, for the latter part of that time she would have to be Stateside to get the required work experience. In the meanwhile, however, she could do her classes from pretty much anywhere on earth where there was an internet connection.

Lind and her husband, having seen their retirement plans upended and the financial security that they had anticipated as they aged evaporate, were trying to make the best of their new reality. If she didn't get a paid job within a couple months of returning from Japan, they were planning to put their possessions into storage and go around the world for nine months, flying first to New Zealand, then onto Australia, from there to several countries in Asia, over to the Mediterranean, north Africa, and finally Ireland before returning Stateside.

In most of these countries, they had plenty of friends, from their decades of overseas service, whom they could stay with. He would birdwatch and catch up on reading all the books that he had wanted to read but, while working, somehow hadn't had the time to. She would study mornings and late evenings. "We are looking for the lemonade wherever we can find it," Lind said. Nearly half a year on from her first being put onto Administrative Leave, she was far more philosophical about her situation than she had initially been. "It's going to be an amalgamation of work and retirement and travel. What we've lost in pension and salary, we've gained in time. We'll do things in our fifties that we had planned to do in our sixties. Time is precious. Gaining time is a really big deal."

Yet, despite her generally calmer frame of mind, when she thought about how she and her colleagues had been treated she could still be roused to fury. She found it hard to fathom how even after she had been placed on Administrative Leave and told she couldn't work, she had been forced to write a weekly performance report. "Having to recall and review what I achieved and will never get credit for was deeply painful," she remembered. The way she looked at it, the sort of work that she had devoted her adult life to was facing "an extinction event," and the people with control over her wages and her retirement benefits were reveling in her distress. "I mentored, counseled and advised dozens of new and aspiring employees," Lind wrote in one of these reports, as she looked back over her recent service with USAID as it went through its death throes. "I served as a sounding board and shoulder for staff that had dreamed of making a career in the Democracy, Rights, and Governance development sector facing the end of that career path." She closed out her report somewhat defiantly: "I supported my colleagues with empathy and respect — that will be my legacy."

Now, from her vantage point across the Pacific Ocean, in Japan, she continued to nurture her anger at Elon Musk. Imagine, she said, how much better the world could have been if Musk "had been raised as a decent human being. He could really have changed things for humanity, and instead he's chosen this path. How mind-boggling that is." When she thought about it, she found that her anger at the world's richest man was more pronounced than that she felt toward Donald Trump. The president, she felt, was a *schnorrer*, a Yiddish insult that, roughly, translates as a not particularly serious human being, a rampant freeloader. He was, she had concluded, someone who did whatever would give him a sense that he was important, that he was powerful. That made him not a towering historical figure but rather a "ridiculous, comical character."

By contrast, Musk, she felt was a smart man with a truly warped set of values. She pondered what she would ask him if she ever had the chance. "Does he see how his influence on the world is for the worse, not the better? Does he see how many people he's hurt and injured and killed? Does that matter to him? As a father, how can he see empathy as a negative human emotion?" Ultimately, she concluded, what she really wanted to know of Musk was, "Who hurt you?"

With Memorial Day nearing, Dan Meleason and his spouse were planning a head-clearing camping trip north to the Grand Teton and Yellowstone national parks. They would, he said, pack up their car with gear, including bear spray and, possibly, an air horn to scare off would-be predators, and, along with their two dogs, set off on something of a spontaneous adventure. Where they would stay each night, he wasn't sure — the plan, if one could call it that, was to simply find a plausible fire road at the end of each day, head down it, and look for camping spots to pitch their tent and cook up their meals. For food, they would take plenty of peanut butter and jelly, protein bars, and easy-to-cook dishes such as spaghetti. They had supplies of coffee and tea and almond milk. How long they would be gone for was also up in the air. So, too, was the final destination. They were both actively thinking about moving to Canada, and, he said, should the mood strike them they would drive over the border and into British Columbia, would check into a hotel in Vancouver, spruce themselves up and reach out to vague contacts he had — connections of connections, as he explained it — to ask about jobs.

Meleason had never been to Yellowstone before, and he was practically bouncing off the walls with excitement as he prepared the trip. That it wasn't rigidly scheduled out, that each day was something of a blank slate, made it that much more exciting. "The end state I don't think is defined," he said.

The ex-cryptologist needed some downtime. He had been paying attention to every twist and every turn in the Trumpian saga for months now, and it wasn't making him particularly happy. True, he felt now that in the five stages of grief he was starting to move toward the fifth, acceptance; but in the grand scheme of things he was still continually amazed by what was happening in the country that he loved. How could Trump play around with the economic well-being of the United States through firing off one irrational social media post after the next, about tariffs, about the federal reserve and its chairman whom he wanted to fire, about inflation, and not expect an economic comeuppance? When, in mid-May, Moody's credit rating agency downgraded US credit, making US bonds a less safe bet than Canadian, Australian, German, Dutch, and British debt, he laughed grimly. Each day, he felt, the administration conjured up another Alice-through-the-looking-glass moment. He looked at the lush green mountain sides of Colorado after a long snow-and-rain season, and saw brush ready to dry out and become fuel for fires later in the year; when the administration talked about opening up the national forests to logging as a fire mitigation strategy, he looked at the steepness of some of the slopes and realized it would be prohibitively expensive to log this land. Come the summer, he knew, dry lightning would strike, or some clod would throw a burning cigarette butt out the car window, and the infernos would start up again — but this time around they would be doing so with fewer expert fire crews on call and less federal money available to assist in firefighting and in recovery efforts.

Meleason considered this to be "ideocracy," a form of short-termism that seemed utterly incapable of considering the long-term consequences of actions. It was, he said, taking root and undermining all the things he deemed important in the body politic. He took solace, however, in the fact that the human story was an old one and that, over the millennia, countries and cultures had waxed and waned in their powers and glories. The United States, he said, was a young country, just approaching its 250th birthday; compared to civilizations that had been around for thousands of years, it was just a Johnny-Come-Lately. Plenty of time both for America to screw things up and for America to eventually right itself again. But, he acknowledged, that process of righting the American ship might take an awfully long time. "The long-term may be one hundred years from now, quite frankly. After we are returned to star dust." His training in the military, he argued, had given him the ability to distinguish between the near-term, tactical or operational mentality and the long-term strategy. It was, he argued, important for people who held democracy dear to think about long-term ways to regain momentum in a country in which democracy appeared in some ways to be stalling out.

Some days, all Meleason wanted to do was to tune out the noise of a chaotic, angry, political moment. But then the engaged citizen in him rejected that approach. "It's irrational to live life with our heads in the sand," he concluded. "Putting blinkers on or rose-colored glasses on doesn't help. You have to understand what's going on in the world to effect change."

Adrian M was spending much of the spring thinking about God — not to avoid engaging with the daily realities of life as a targeted federal employee, but rather to better contextualize what was happening.

The total of jobs she had applied for was now approaching two hundred, and she still hadn't gotten any offers. Increasingly, she would submit her résumé, adjusted to meet the requirements of the job, only to receive word back that the job listing had been withdrawn due to a lack of funds. She was, in real time, witnessing a domino effect, with the withdrawal of federal funds collapsing local and state public health funding systems, as well as those of healthcare non-profits.

To ease the gnawing anxiety that increasingly afflicted her, Adrian was studying the Bible — the Book of Job, detailing the concept of unmerited suffering, was her current favorite reading; she was attending YouTube services for her hometown church in Tennessee, the Bethel Christian Church; and was watching daily TikTok broadcasts by a lay priest that provided viewers with both a "Daily Devotional" and a guided prayer. Her TikTok algorithm knew her well enough at this point to continually feed her new gospel music and videos of people in prayer.

Adrian viewed her relationship with God very personally. She prayed that funding would be restored to the CDC, and she prayed that she would find a decently paying job and would continue to be able to afford her monthly bills. Increasingly, she prayed that those who abused Christian tenets by claiming that their faith gave them the right to inflict fire and brimstone on their political foes, or to take away people's employment, or to deny children nutritional assistance would face some sort of comeuppance. "I'm definitely a believer in karma," she explained. "They're going to crash and burn, because they're doing dirty." She viewed Trump as being a false idol, and took comfort from Luke 10:19, in which believers were told, "Behold, I give you the authority to trample on any serpents and scorpions;" she viewed Trump and his administration as the scorpions and serpents, and an outraged electorate as the vessel that would eventually bring them down to earth. "You can't use Jesus to justify doing wrong, doing bad and evil things," she averred.

Adrian M was on numerous Signal chats with other vulnerable federal employees. The volume of messages could be overwhelming. She'd take a mental health break for a few hours or even days and find that she had to catch up on several hundred messages. "People are trauma-dumping in some of the Signal chats," she observed. "And then everyone starts feeding off of the anxiety and off of the stress." There was the story of the ex-CDC scientist now working at a Starbucks to make ends meet. There were stories of people being so traumatized they couldn't concentrate enough to work. Adrian herself had decided to postpone necessary house repairs, because she was nervous that she wouldn't be able to cover the costs.

She struggled to come up with an analogy to describe the impact, both on federal employees and on the community at large, of the massive cuts to public health expenditures. Finally, she hit on one: public health was about waging a war against disease and against the conditions of poverty and inequality in which diseases and preventable injuries were most likely to occur, and now the public health warriors were being told they had to lay down their weapons and retreat from the field. Entire offices, from the Office of Smoking Health to the Division of Population Health, were being shredded. Campaigns against domestic violence were being stopped in their tracks. Injury prevention programs were being defunded.

Downwind, states were facing huge losses to their public health budgets — Georgia, alone, the state in which the CDC was headquartered, was facing a loss of $344 million as a direct consequence of the Reduction-In-Force* order. And, once the GOP-led Congress passed a budget, the size of those cuts would grow even more.

Federal regulations on basic safety issues such as the standards that had to apply to car seats were being rolled back to the states — meaning that states such as California, with strong regulatory systems, would continue to mandate the sale of high-quality car seats, but many other states, lacking both the political will and the economic resources, would likely cease to enforce standards that reached the level the federal government had previously adhered to. "That means children are going to die, because their car seats are not regulated at a federal level," Adrian believed.

Ultimately, for Adrian, what was happening in 2025 represented a stunning surrender in the fight against disease and against injuries caused by faulty products. "When you dismantle the army, nobody's fighting the war anymore."

The letters sent by the Acting General Counsel to the United States Department of Commerce were hardly designed to mollify Kelsey Hendrix's anger at how she had been treated. On April 10, she was abruptly informed that the temporary restraining order that had reinstated her was now no longer in effect. "Accordingly, the Department is reverting your termination action to its original effective date," John Guenther wrote. "The Department will waive any indebtedness created by the court's order that you be paid beyond your termination date." Guenther's follow up letter, from May 7, was so grumpy, Hendrix noted, that all she could do was laugh out loud at its churlishness. The first couple paragraphs bemoaned the fact that Judge Alsup had required that the department write to each fired employee individually, informing them that their termination was not "'performance" or fitness based." The third paragraph said the Department believed the judge's order to be factually erroneous and was appealing it. And the fourth paragraph begrudgingly stated that "the Department of Commerce hereby informs you, as required by the Court, that your earlier termination 'was not "performance" or fitness based but was made as part of a government-wide mass termination.'"

By now, Hendrix had decided that, even if and when she got a new job, she would continue to fight her case against the feds. It was, she said, just simply wrong to falsely accuse her of poor performance, when she had a documented track record of stellar performance; it would make it almost impossible to get re-hired by the feds down the road. Hendrix was a part of ongoing class-action lawsuits against the firings. She had also consulted an attorney about going it alone with her appeal. "It's the principle of the matter. I'm not going to let some dumdum and his band of whatevers tarnish my reputation and all of our reputations," she said, with a touch of the braggadocio that had gotten the blind woman through life so far. "I don't appreciate bullies, and they're being bullies." Hendrix was disillusioned by how many political figures had simply kissed Trump's ring rather than stand up for what she assumed they knew in their hearts was right. By contrast, she was overjoyed whenever a federal judge handed down a ruling curtailing at least some of the administration's abuses. "They are awesome," she gushed, "and I wish I could send them all donuts. Or fruit baskets. Or literally anything to show our appreciation of them."

For the past month, since the RIF notice had come down, Hendrix had devoted hours a day to applying for jobs. She would spend as much time as she could bear searching the internet for listings; and, when her brain started to spin with exhaustion, would then take some downtime playing the Slay the Spire video game, or listening to television, the audio assist function narrating to her what was going on on the screen that she could not see. "Probably definitely," she was listening to more TV than she had when she had a job.

Hendrix didn't deal with boredom well. When she wasn't working, she felt that her brain was starting to atrophy. She got frustrated easily, and then would come the sadness, the fixation on how many workers had had their lives thrown into chaos and how many vital government programs were now grinding to a halt. She talked about people she knew with cancer who had lost their health insurance. She thought of co-workers who had spent years developing special skills needed only in the federal government, and who would, in a saturated job market, struggle to find work.

By the late spring, she had decided to stop speaking with her grandparents, infuriated at what she considered to be their tactless defense of Trump and of the DOGE cuts, and at what she felt was their assertion that maybe she should reconsider her career and find more "productive" work outside of government. Even on her grandmother's birthday, she didn't phone her. She *was* still speaking with her mother, but they studiously avoided touching on politics. That people she loved had drunk the Kool-Aid filled her with horror. She loathed bigotry, but she could understand, sort of, how one group could be convinced to hate another group who differed from them in the color of their skin, or their national origin or their religion. What she couldn't understand was the rage directed at federal workers whose jobs involved finding cures for diseases or warning people about impending weather disasters or devoting long hours to make workplaces safer for workers. "This I do not understand," she admitted. "It would be like me hating a fireman: 'how dare you go into that burning building and save lives?!' It makes no sense." Hendrix had long stopped being religious, but every so often her Evangelical roots burst through. She no longer believed in the Devil, but she said, if she was wrong and Satan did exist, well he was sure doing a good job via the machinations of DOGE.

To fill in the gaps in her schedule and to minimize the time she spent obsessing, Hendrix had begun volunteering with a local mutual assistance group, working on their food and clothing drives, and helping to set up a free legal clinic for immigrants facing the full force of the new administration's crackdowns. She had also started volunteering, remotely, for a cat rescue organization in Pennsylvania, screening people who wanted to adopt one of the pets. It was far enough way that, her boyfriend half-joked, she couldn't be tempted to herself bring home one of the abandoned animals.

The ex-NOAA worker had also started learning Spanish again, on Duolingo, hoping to address a regret she had had for years — that she hadn't kept up her Spanish language skills after graduating from high school. It wasn't coming easy — despite weeks of practice, she was still on section one, cramming basic verb tenses and re-learning elementary conversational skills, such as how to ask for directions in an unfamiliar city.

Some Tuesdays, she went over to Congress with other fired federal workers to meet up with Congress members. She had been lucky enough, she said giddily, to go into Senator Cory Booker's office the second day of his record-breaking 25-hour speech protesting the Trump administration's actions, and to be offered by one of his assistants a gallery pass that allowed her to sit in on his speech for several hours. It was the first time she had ever been into the gallery of the Senate before, and it left her with goosebumps. "It was really cool," she gushed. "We got to be there and witness history."

Following an initial drought, she had started hearing back from potential employers, and by mid-May was being asked in for a number of interviews, both with private sector companies and for state jobs in Maryland. One interview, in particular, for a procurement officer's position, had left her on a high; it had been an in-person interview, and she had spent time exploring the government building and its elegant courtyard, piecing together mental images of her surroundings through the sounds, touch and smell of the place. "The fresh air, you can smell it, feel it. Outside sounds. I use those to put together a picture. I don't know if it's visually accurate, but it gives me a good sense of what is physically around."

Hendrix hadn't yet heard back from any of the interviews and was all-too-aware that she was competing against scores of other federal employees for the few open jobs in her specialty area. But she had had one piece of good luck. Weeks earlier, she had enrolled in a research study being conducted by Georgetown University neurologists that involved doing MRIs of the brains of people who had been born blind. She had worn one of her NOAA T shirts to the lab, and when the scientist conducting the experiments had asked her about her work at NOAA, she had told her that she was a DOGE victim. Her story stuck with the woman, and sometime later, when a part time outreach job opened up, that involved finding people to take part in experiments the lab was conducting, the scientist reached out to Hendrix to see if she'd be interested in it. It wouldn't pay much — somewhere in the thirty-five dollar an hour range for a handful of hours a week — but Hendrix viewed it as a start and leaped at the opportunity. "I will take it over unemployment. It's something," she decided. "At the very least, it will make my savings last longer." She was hoping to start working in early June.

Meanwhile, her search for more stable, full-time employment continued apace. "It's demoralizing to apply for jobs hours and hours a day," she admitted. But, she said, she refused to succumb to that demoralization. She had fashioned for herself a new motto, one that she felt summed up her attitude to life. "I'm trying to stave off the boredom, make a difference, and not lose my apartment." As the summer of 2025 got underway, that was as good a pledge that the fired NOAA procurement officer could make to herself as any other.

With the cool days of early spring giving way to the heat of June, Carmen Drier was engaged in what they called a "war of attrition" with the feds. Their bosses at the Department of the Interior were trying to make life as miserable as possible for the environmental scientists, hoping that, even if the courts temporarily blocked the wholesale firing of staff, they could render the workplace so unendurable that, in their droves, staff would quit.

For Drier, that was an action of last resort. "They're trying to get me to surrender, and I'm like, 'you'll have to kill me first,'" they said, only half-joking. Quit, and they wouldn't be eligible for state unemployment benefits. Hang around long enough to get the feds to fire them, and those benefits would then kick in. Drier was on a yearly contract — the sort that, in normal years, was automatically rolled over barring misconduct on the part of the employee. 2025 wasn't a normal year, however, and with broad hiring freezes in place contract employees were being let loose when their yearly contracts expired. Drier was fully expecting that when their contract ended in late August, it wouldn't be renewed.

Meanwhile, the drumbeat of unpleasant news continued. In mid-May, rumors had flown that upwards of 1,000 staff at the National Park Service, and hundreds more at the US Geological Survey, the Bureau of Land Management, and the

Fish and Wildlife Service would be RIF'ed. In agencies throughout government, climate scientists, environmental scientists,
and environmental justice researchers were being fired. A colleague had dryly remarked in the office, "I hope I don't get fired
before the rest of the roses bloom." Another had observed that
the cruelest part of the whole process was not knowing from
one day to the next whether one had a job — and finding out
not via official channels but on social media or on the news that
your office was up next for the chopping block. Scientists were
in a "mad panic" to publish their research findings before their
jobs were cut and they were blocked from being able to upload
data onto government websites.

By May, so few IT people were left in the office that, on the days
that e-waste was supposed to be picked up, the one remaining
staffer physically couldn't lift all the machines down to the bins
and had to call on Drier, themselves not much taller than five
feet, to help her.

On a near-daily basis, Carmen Drier wondered if any of this
was worth it. Their parents back East had told them to just
do whatever made sense; their friends would go out for drinks
with them and offer words of condolence for the situation —
almost as if someone had died. Each interaction made Drier
feel, somehow, guilty, as if they had done something wrong.
"They ask, 'how are you doing?' It's extremely awkward and
I feel like I'm doing something wrong to my friends by not
knowing where I'll be at the end of the summer." Yet, when
they thought about applying for other jobs, it seemed entirely
overwhelming — especially given that the jobs that appealed to

Drier tended to be with non-profit conservation groups, which were exactly the sorts of organizations now losing federal grants at a rapid clip. "I should be looking for another job," the young researcher acknowledged. "I shouldn't feel burned out. But I feel prevented from looking for another job, because if I don't have the motivation for something it's very difficult to spend hours on these applications when I'm so depressed about my skills and my goals."

Increasingly, Drier felt that they were back in the Covid lockdowns, cut off from the rest of the world. But this time, the culprit wasn't a virus, it was the federal administration. They were resorting to coping mechanisms that had got them through the darkest days of the pandemic — spending more time talking to friends, reading as much as possible, watching bad reality TV shows. "Yes, things are kind of shit," they told themself, "but you just have to laugh and focus on what you can do. Because it's just a rolling train, you know. Trump hates me and he hates everyone I love. It's kind of crazy."

The reverse road trip wasn't nearly as fun for Natasha Miles as her trip out west in February had been.

After realizing that she couldn't afford to stay in Colorado indefinitely, Miles had finally made the call to Penn State to see if there was a way she could get her old job back. It turned out there was; while one of the main projects she had been working on, involving taking carbon dioxide and methane readings from a number of cell phone towers dotted around Indianapolis, had had its funding pulled, another emissions-reading project, this one funded by NASA and in collaboration with the jet propulsion laboratory, was somehow still a go, and it needed a scientist with Miles' particular skills.

She packed her bags and boxes and suitcases into her car again, dumped her skis and other sports paraphernalia atop them, readied her dog, Mia, for the long ride, and, on April 29, set off home. She'd been in Boulder such a short time that neither of her sons had yet had time to come out and visit her and to see, for the first time, the magnificent Rockies. On the way west, in the dead of winter, she had veered south on the I-70 through Kansas; this time around she went the northern route, along the I-80. A night in a small town along the interstate in Nebraska, another in Iowa, stopping every few hours to let Mia stretch her legs. A side trip to the shores of the Mississippi River. A few days with her husband in Champaign, Illinois. And then a two-and-a-half-hour jag east again to her parents' home in Indiana, where she decamped for a week to help her mother recover from surgery.

On the evening of May 10, Miles arrived back at the house in Pennsylvania that she had, fortuitously, decided not to sell at the start of the year. It was the eve of Mother's Day. The next afternoon, her sons — both at the university, the oldest readying himself for a summer internship, the youngest working at a local restaurant — would take her out to lunch at a local Mexican restaurant, and she would celebrate with a plate of enchiladas.

Other than that, though, she felt there was precious little to be festive about. True, she knew she was lucky to have a job and a pay-check — and to have finally managed, a few weeks earlier, to get on her husband's health insurance and to start taking again full doses of the drugs that she needed to control her Crohn's Disease. That, at least, was a burden she no longer had to carry. But she knew that her new job — reliant as it was on federal grant money — could disappear at any moment, and she worried that the country was, by the minute, becoming more hostile to climate science.

When she had moved into her studio in the mountains above Boulder, she had wanted to make it seem like home. To tuck things away, to hang things up. Now, she couldn't even bring herself to unpack. "Anything that I didn't need immediately is still piled up in boxes and bags and such," she admitted some weeks later. She thought about putting it all in closets and cupboards, but then she realized that the Penn State project might go belly-up any day and that, in consequence, she would have to move on again in the not-too-distant future. Miles had kept her options open regarding the project in France that she had expressed interest in joining earlier in the spring, and she was hoping to hear more from them in the next month or two. A small part of her still hoped against hope that her job at NOAA would somehow be resurrected, though as she watched the budget negotiations unfold in Congress between different wings of the Republican Party, she had to accept the cold facts that the choices facing the workers in her field were somewhere between awful and catastrophic. Another part of her recognized the possibility that she would have to apply for any and every job in her field that became available in the US — and that that might entail her moving to yet another state.

As someone who had studied CO_2 and methane emissions for decades, Miles was particularly depressed at the wrecking of any and all climate change-related federal projects and data measuring protocols. She saw an Administration contemptuous of science and interested only in the short-terms financial gains embodied in their "drill, baby, drill" mantra. "If we're going to mitigate risk, we need to reduce our emissions, and that's not really where we're headed right now," she acknowledged. "It's going to increase the risks from climate change even more so. It's going to be hard to avoid disastrous impacts. It's going to be disastrous not just for the US but for the whole world."

After years in which it finally seemed that the country had turned a corner and was effectively engaging with the escalating climate crisis, now everything had been jolted into reverse. "I'm still feeling kind of in shock that all of this has happened," she acknowledged. "Even though it's been three months since I was originally fired. It's surreal that this has happened."

By late May, the legal battle over the mass firings of federal workers and the *de facto* dismantling of Congressionally-mandated and funded government agencies and bureaus was picking up steam. Several judges had handed down rulings, in response to lawsuits brought by government employees and their unions, finding the process to have been carried out illegally. In consequence, a growing number of workers were being brought back into the offices from which they had either been fired or placed on Administrative Leave weeks or months earlier.

Oftentimes, however, there seemed precious little rhyme or reason to the decisions. Where once there had been offices effectively staffed to meet their needs, now there were islands of employees in otherwise still-shuttered facilities. In some cases, even when the government made an effort to reinstate workers, they found those workers had moved on, either accepting the fork in the road offer, retiring, or finding other jobs. In other cases, reinstatement letters only went out to a select few employees.

In mid-May, Hannah Echt and approximately 300 other NIOSH staff received email notices abruptly informing them that their Administrative Leave was over and that they were expected to report back to work. The National Firefighter Registry for studying firefighters' vulnerability to cancer was being restored; so too was the black lung surveillance program for coal miners, the registry monitoring the use of personal protective equipment in workplaces, and the Health Hazard Evaluation Program that Echt worked for. Yet numerous other programs weren't being restored, and many of the back-up staff the restored programs needed in order to function effectively had likewise been left on the chopping block: over the coming weeks, Echt would realize that while she could conduct workplace visits and take samples of potentially toxic materials, once she returned to her still largely empty office she would struggle to get those samples analyzed, since many of NIOSH's chemists remained on Administrative Leave.

Gingerly, the NIOSH crews began dipping their toes into the work-waters again, feeling out what they could and couldn't do, what would or wouldn't be funded. They didn't know if their workplace credit cards were going to be restored, or whether they would be allowed to travel for work — a necessity given the investigations their office was responsible for were geographically dispersed in workplaces around the country. What astounded Echt was the amount of red tape she faced; after all, part of the ostensible rationale that Trump and Musk had pushed for why they were taking their chain saw to government was that they were rolling back decades of accumulated, and needless, regulations. Yet here the NIOSH staff were, in mid-2025, having to jump through hoops just to get approved to go on workplace site visits that, six months earlier, would simply have been standard operating procedure.

A few days before Memorial Day, Echt used some of her vacation leave to journey, with dozens of her fellow NIOSH workers from Cincinnati, Morgantown, and Pittsburgh, on an AFL-CIO-provided bus to DC. For weeks, since well before any of them were reinstated, they had been planning a lobby day in the nation's capital followed, the next morning, by a lively protest outside the Health and Human Services headquarters to push for the restoring of NIOSH's functions. As a union steward, there was never any doubt in Echt's mind about whether she should still go.

The NIOSH workers donned dark blue T shirts, embossed with white wording. On the front of these shirts was written "NIOSH: Protecting Workers Since 1970"; on the back, "Science for the working people." Some groups, including Echt's, visited the staff of Democratic lawmakers — Echt talked with Virginia Senator Tim Kaine's staff, as well as those of representatives from Connecticut and from the Chicago suburbs; others chose to tackle Republicans, making a point to stop by to talk with elected officials from coal-mining states such as West Virginia, pushing their point that NIOSH worked for all Americans, regardless of their political affiliations.

At the rally the next morning, on what was otherwise a chilly and rain-soaked day, the sun came out just long enough for one hundred NIOSH workers and their allies to state their piece. The president of the coal miners' union took the bullhorn to address the crowd; so, too, did representatives of the steelworkers' and nurses' unions. Toward the end of the event, Echt herself gathered up her nerves, breathed deep to tamp down the anxiety that, throughout her life had welled up at inconvenient moments, and spoke to her colleagues. She talked about the vital work that her team did and the workers who were protected as a result. By the time it was over, and they were ready to start on the 11-hour bus ride back through Morgantown, Pittsburgh, and onto Cincinnati, Echt was exhausted, "But, like, a good tired," she explained. "It made a difference and helped morale a lot too. I don't think we've entirely won yet. But we've definitely gotten a victory. It's awesome."

The following evening, Echt and her fiancé celebrated — just a little — by ordering Italian takeout, a shrimp pasta for her, a chicken marsala for him, and, with glasses of Seven and Seven whiskey cocktails in hand, curling up on the couch to watch an animated movie.

The next few months would, they knew, be particularly hectic. They had nailed down their wedding date and, a few days previously, just before Echt returned to work, had mailed out the invites. At least in part to make up for the fact that both of Echt's older siblings had married during the pandemic and were unable to hold large celebratory parties (Echt's brother had tied the knot in a ceremony that she and others had attended on Zoom) they had decided to hold a big shindig, at a Carnegie Center in town that had previously been a library but now was serving as a community hub for weddings and other events. They had, she estimated, sent out invites to more than 130 people and were hopeful that their nuptials would serve to get most-everyone they loved together. Now, they were turning their attention to the honeymoon; they wanted to spend time on the west coast, in Portland and Seattle. What they hadn't decided yet was whether to fly or to take Amtrak trains west, meandering across the country for a few days *en route* to visit his uncle and aunt in Portland and her old UW stomping grounds in Seattle.

Between now and then, Echt was planning to stay loud and to use her role as a union steward to explain to as many people as possible just how important was the work that NIOSH was supposed to be doing. She was under no illusions that the members of the administration had suddenly had a kumbaya moment and were restoring several hundred NIOSH workers out of the goodness of their hearts. Rather, they were doing so in part because the courts were forcing their hands, and in part, too, because the NIOSH workforce had been particularly effective in selling their case to members of Congress and to the general public. And that was the biggest incentive Echt could imagine to keep on raising her voice. "We just got a tangible win with the small number of people who were brought back," she said. "It's more motivation for us to keep doing what we're doing."

Others weren't so lucky. After he and his brother had returned from Germany, Ed Brisbane found himself at a loose end. He had never been a big reader — a few Harry Potter books in high school, some *Game of Thrones* volumes in college. Now, he found that he had no desire to pick up any books. Instead, he scrolled his phone and spent hours each day sitting on his four-seat blue couch and watching movies or playing video games with his brother. Some days, he would realize at day's end that he had spent upwards of five hours on his computer console. He tried to get in regular runs, went to the gym to pump weights — he also kept 35-pound dumbbells on his carpeted living room floor — and every so often played some pick-up basketball. Weekends, he, his twin brother, as well as their older brother would work for the cruise company, and, after they had checked the passengers in, would go off to a restaurant by the docks to eat a meal. But even so, he felt like he had no goals. "I liked working for the IRS," he explained. "I'm helping the government, serving the public." He had become, he realized, job proud. "I've never lived in a city, never worked in a city. It felt cool, felt official that I was working downtown — having a steady, good job, contributing to society. I definitely wanted to help them [taxpayers whom he talked with over the phone], for sure."

In the first days after he and his brother had been fired, neither of them spoke about it with their family or friends. Brisbane felt sheepish, almost ashamed, as if he must have done something wrong. "It felt a little humiliating to have to leave," he realized. He knew that most of his friends didn't read the news very closely and weren't aware of the mass firings that were going on. Were he tell them that he had been kicked out of his job, he feared they would simply assume it was his fault.

During and after the Germany trip, however, he had let more of his friends into his secret — and had found out that at least some of them were as angry as was he at what was happening. One of his friends, an avid outdoorsman, was livid at the decimation of the National Park Service. Another simply couldn't stand Elon Musk and Donald Trump. Yet many of his friends seemed to care less about the broader political story and more about his personal situation: they were jealous that he was being paid to loll about and play video games until September. Brisbane could see their point; he wasn't, he said, in any hurry to apply for jobs, since he didn't have a family to support or a mortgage to pay, and his income was secure at least through the summer. At that point, he surmised, he would look for other work — hopefully a job putting his skills to use in state or local government. Meanwhile, instead of having to get up at 6:15 each morning, he could sleep through until 9 or 10 a.m., have a leisurely breakfast, and then play video games all day. When he got bored of the games, he said, if he had nothing else to do he would just power through the boredom, playing even more games on his computer to while away the hours. Evenings, when they weren't out with their friends, Ed Brisbane and his brother would cook at home, simple meals, heavy on meat and light on vegetables. Explaining his avoidance of legumes, he said simply, "They don't taste good."

Most days, that routine seemed to just about get him through until nightfall — at which point, he would scroll on his phone again until, eventually, he tired. His life, at times, seemed to come down to a series of interactions with miscellaneous screens.

Some days, on one screen or another, he half-heartedly browsed job listings or enrolled in virtual job fairs. Brisbane had hopes that down the road he would find another good position, with the promise of security and decent benefits. He thought it increasingly unlikely, however, that it would be a federal job, and he felt a growing sense of anger at the vandalism unleashed against the civil service not by Trump — whom he viewed some-what as the junior partner in all of this — but by Elon Musk.

If he met Musk, Brisbane steamed, "I would be pissed at him. I'd ask him why he's firing good people, why he's lying about their performance, how is this efficient. I'd ask why he's a bil-lionaire and he's firing people making not a ton of money. I'd ask how it's helping, for sure. I'd ask why he doesn't tell people that he's paying people to do nothing. I'd ask why he hates nor-mal people, government workers. I'd ask how he thinks it's fair to fire people with families, who can't get jobs in this market. And I'd ask how it's good for the country."

Brisbane's instinctual conservatism had, over these months, been replaced by something else — by a sense of omnipresent distrust at a broken system. Whichever way he looked, it seemed as if powerful political figures were stiffing people like him. "It feels like our whole government is screwed up at this point," he opined. "I feel like our whole government is compromised, which sucks."

Daniel Dodd-Ramirez felt much the same way. He had, by late May just about had it with his new bosses at what was left of the Consumer Financial Protection Bureau. For the past four months, the offices had been shuttered, with workers only allowed in for scheduled meetings if they had been pre-approved by leadership and had their names put onto a thumb's up list at the security desk in the lobby. It made even the semblance of work that, in the face of court orders to preserve the bureau, the Administration had, reluctantly, eventually been forced to allow workers to carry out, little more than a farce.

The new leaders claimed that they had had to introduce these security protocols to protect DOGE officials roaming the building from being harassed by angry workers. Daniel was convinced the real reason was far more nefarious. "This leadership intends to abolish the agency. Musk said RIP CFPB after his DOGE officials entered our building, and Trump has said the same. This is one small example on a long list of actions which they have taken to torment Federal workers and keep us from our important work of serving the public."

What Dodd-Ramirez couldn't stop thinking about was that his agency was working to prevent ordinary Americans being taken financial advantage of by large and well-heeled corporations. And, for that sin, it was being destroyed. Meanwhile, on a daily basis, what he saw as the open corruption of the new

Administration picked up steam. There were stories in the news about the Department of Justice closing down anti-corruption units; enforcement of the Foreign Corrupt Practices Act had, by order of the White House, been iced; the president had accepted a half billion dollar jet from the Qatari government to use as a luxury new Air Force One; and Trump had, recently, hosted a private dinner for the top contributors to his $TRUMP meme-coin venture. The pay-to-play schemes were unprecedented in modern American history. "You go into a job feeling purpose and wanting to give back to the country, and then you're treated like this by half the country believing you are this lazy criminal. And the person telling them this *is* the lazy criminal." He laughed bitterly. "It really is ironic. I don't feel disgust or shock anymore. I just feel resignation at this point. The crypto stuff is especially poignant, because it is in our wheelhouse."

Dodd-Ramirez also couldn't get over the number of top business figures willing to kiss the ring in meetings with Trump. He and his colleagues had spent years fighting corruption, and now, even as they were being ordered to cease their work, they were seeing what were at best sordid interactions between top business and political figures virtually institutionalized.

On a daily basis, more and more of Dodd-Ramirez's colleagues had accepted a deferred resignation or opted to retire. Others were taking state jobs in locales around the country. At the rare work meetings they still held, the remaining staff expressed their growing fury at the way they were being treated and at the financial uncertainties they were now facing in consequence. Those survivors — and Daniel counted himself among them, having decided to sweat it out as long as possible in his own personal protest at the wrongness of what the Administration was doing — were living the trauma that Russell Vought had vowed to inflict on the federal workforce. Daniel himself had grown resigned to the CFPB's evisceration and talked of federal workers' spirits being crushed by the avalanche of actions directed against them. "It is very sad," he wrote in late May, "but there is nothing more that we can do."

Now, Dodd-Ramirez was, too, finally making a conscious effort to move on. He was in conversation with a couple non-profits about jobs — they would pay about half of what he was currently making, but he figured that with the pension and healthcare benefits the government would owe him if they forced him into early retirement from the CFPB, he would just about be able to swing it. He had, once again, had to postpone his forty-five-day silent meditation retreat, but he was hoping to negotiate with his new employers leave for early 2026 so that he could finally go on retreat and clear his head of all the unpleasantness that had accumulated over the first half of 2025. "I feel I have to move on," he concluded. "I've done everything I could, and this is really out of our control."

EPILOGUE

In late May, Kelsey Hendrix wrote me a long note from her home in a multistory apartment building north of downtown Washington, *DC.* She was, she explained, "just tired. My heart hurts for the people who will suffer because of the cuts to NWS [the National Weather Service] and other NOAA programs, as well as the life-saving work of other employees at USAID and other agencies who are no longer there to do their jobs. I wonder what kind of world our babies are going to grow up in. I worry for people who live in areas more likely to be hit by hurricanes, tornadoes, and other natural disasters who won't have aid or warnings in time. I'm concerned for everyone currently trying to figure out how to make enough money to keep food on the table and roofs over our heads."

The ex-NOAA worker still nurtured what she called a "simmering rage" at how she and her colleagues had been treated, and, more generally, at the fact that so much vital work was now not being done — leaving the American population more vulnerable to everything from extreme weather to preventable diseases. She had largely stopped talking to her parents and grandparents, unable to stay quiet in the face of their ongoing defense of Donald Trump and his agenda. Every day, she feared that the DOGE cuts would once again accelerate and that additional tranches of federal workers would find themselves on the scrap heap.

Hendrix's fears were backed up by hard numbers. In early June, the Labor Department estimated that the federal government's payroll had shrunk by 22,000 just in the month of May alone. And by July, the non-profit Partnership for Public Service would estimate that 148,000 federal workers had either resigned, been laid off, or been fired during the first six months of Trump's second administration. Other estimates ranged far higher. Moreover, there was no end in sight to the federal carnage. To the contrary, the plans to shrink government were only accelerating; indeed, in the spring the *New York Times* reported that the Administration intended to reduce the size of the federal workforce by another 150,000 people over the months to come.

And yet, Hendrix continued, she refused to let this grim era defeat her. Even in her bleakest moments, she made a point of at least once a day grabbing her cane from where she hung it on hooks on her front door, shouting out to her three cats, Miles, Simba and Ellie, that she was leaving, heading to the elevator and descending to the lobby level. As she heard each of the building employees' voices, she greeted them by name, accepted their help in guiding her through the heavy glass exit doors, and then headed off for a short walk around her neighborhood, her long, wavy dark hair blowing in the breeze. There was something irrepressibly upbeat about her, something epitomized by the large treble clef she had had tattooed high up on the left side of her chest. Friends would ask her why, when she couldn't see it, she would go to all the bother of getting a tattoo. And she would tell them how she had always loved music, from being a "band geek" in high school through to learning the guitar and, more recently, tinkling on a little keyboard that she and her boyfriend kept in the corner of their living room. When they would press her specifically on the tattoo, she would respond, "I don't know, I like them, it's a different way of expressing myself."

Hendrix was an effusive correspondent and conversationalist, bubbling over with an unstoppable desire to tell her story. She had gotten some more temporary employment, doing contracting work at a military base a 45-minute paratransit ride from her home, and was interviewing for a couple positions with the Maryland state government. She was determined that she would, like her cats, land on her feet. "I'm an optimist by nature: hope for the best, prepare for the worst," she explained. "This is not my first crisis, it won't be my last crisis."

"Though living in the upside down has brought out the worst in some, it has brought out the best in others. This is the hope I cling to when the doom spiral starts," she wrote in her letter. "The government didn't just illegally fire a bunch of random people. They fired employees who decided to dedicate our lives to, in a myriad of different ways, making the lives of other humans better. We are also people who have had it drilled into our heads since the day we took the oath of office that we are a team, not just individual people, and that everyone has an equally important part to play on that team."

The ex-NOAA worker wanted the world to know that she and her colleagues were resilient. "If we all work together and play to our strengths, we just might get through this and come out the other side better. This administration seeks to divide us. They want to make it seem as though we are all alone, and it's an every man for himself situation. This is only true if we let it be true. If we want a better world, we have to make it better."

Hendrix believed that hope would, in the end, win out over all of the fear and division being sown by the Administration, and that the camaraderie-in-pain shown by her colleagues was forging powerful new bonds of community. "They can't stop us from hoping and they can't stop us from helping each other. As it stands, it's not illegal for me to lend a helping hand."

She signed off her letter with a final observation. "The only bad option is sitting back and waiting for someone else to do something instead."

* * *

As the summer got underway, the attacks on federal workers accelerated. In a series of rulings, bitterly opposed by the three liberal Justices on the court, the US Supreme Court cleared the way for the mass firings and RIFs to be implemented; and, a few weeks later, a panel of Ninth Circuit appeals court judges upheld the Trump administration's efforts to end collective bargaining rights for over a million workers — making it even harder for unions to step in to protect at-risk employees. In quick order, entire branches of government were, in practice, eliminated. Amongst the damage: thousands of Department of Education employees were fired; the entire scientific research arm of the Environmental Protection Agency was killed off, resulting in hundreds of chemists, biologists, climate change specialists and others losing their jobs; and, faced with the federal government withdrawing all funding for public broadcasting, the

Congressionally-created Corporation for Public Broadcasting was dissolved.

The attacks on federal employees were in part ideological — the Administration was determined to shut down any work on climate change, was looking to neutralize agencies that enforced workers' rights, and had pledged to its base that it would roll back federal involvement in education and in funding the arts. But they were also deeply personal, with Trump wielding absolute powers to fire people whom he, or his influencer-advisers such as Laura Loomer, deemed weren't sufficiently loyal to his MAGA agenda.

Throughout the summer, Loomer was to be seen wondering the halls of the White House, delivering lists to the Administration of public officials whose loyalty was thought to be suspect. In an interview with *Politico*, the young influencer explained, "I'm happy to take people's tips about disloyal appointees, disloyal staffers, and Biden holdovers. And I guess you could say that my tip line has come to serve as a form of therapy for Trump administration officials who want to expose their colleagues who should not be in the positions that they're in." At the Pentagon, officials began forcing colleagues to take lie detector tests to see who was leaking information. At the Justice Department, by mid-year hundreds of career officials had been fired, many of them for apparently not being loyal enough to Trump's anti-immigration agenda or for having played rolls in the prosecutions of the January 6, 2021, insurrectionists, or of Trump himself.

Six months into his second presidency, Trump was behaving less like the head of a constitutional system of government and more like a capricious monarch. After the Bureau of Labor Statistics released a report showing that job creation had sharply slowed in the late spring and early summer, the head of the bureau was summarily fired by Trump, who took to social media to say that she had manipulated the numbers with the specific intent of making him look bad.

* * *

In late June, just days before Taly Lind and her USAID colleagues were to be terminated from federal employment, Kenneth Jackson, whose email signature somewhat obscurely proclaimed that he was "Performing the Duties of USAID Deputy Administrator for Management and Resources," sent out a note to the USAID staff. It praised them for embodying "the highest standards of public service," and announced that "Your extraordinary efforts have not gone unnoticed. We thank you for your contributions and your commitment." After a few more paragraphs of anodyne double-talk, Jackson's email wrapped up. "From the entire leadership team at USAID, we thank you for your dedication and your service on behalf of our great Nation."

On Substack, many of the USAID employees responded with bitter humor. Parodying Jackson's note, one wrote "As we approach the July 1 liquidation, I want to extend my deepest appreciation for your unwavering service to USAID — even as we dismantle it in broad daylight, without anesthesia, to satisfy the whims of a demolition crew disguised as reformers. Your resolve in navigating the erasure of one of America's most consequential global institutions has not gone unnoticed — especially by those who designed its destruction... Through furloughs, misinformation, and manufactured chaos, you upheld standards this administration long ago abandoned." The satirical letter went on to thank the fired USAID workers for their service "and for trusting, wrongly, that this administration would honor your collective bargaining rights."

At exactly 5 p.m. on Tuesday, July 1, as Taly Lind's months of Administrative Leave ended and she was, finally, severed from government service, Lind sent a final communique to the entire USAID employee list serve. She knew that it likely wouldn't ever be received, as her government clearance had been revoked the second that her contract was terminated, but it made her feel better to say it anyway. "Those of us who have worked in closing political spaces know that it is a roller coaster of losses and wins," Lind wrote. "As our own democracy hits a low and a wave of cruelty, selfishness, and unchecked power hits us, while falsely claiming savings for the American People, we know better."

The about-to-be-unemployed foreign service employee wrote that "America can't be GREAT, if we're not GOOD!" And then she signed off.

That same day, a Tesla Cybertruck hauling a woodchipper in southwestern Colorado caught fire and set the surrounding grasslands ablaze. Taly Lind read the story and, remembering Elon Musk's boast that he had fed USAID into the woodchipper, couldn't help but laugh. It was, she wrote me on Signal as she prepared for the first evening of her post-USAID life, "the perfect metaphor" for what was going on in Trump's America.

ACKNOWLEDGEMENTS

For more than thirty years, I have written columns, feature articles, and books on the great issues confronting American politics and community. Along the way, I have been buoyed by thousands of interactions with men and women around the country, people who have entrusted me to tell their stories. This book is no different; it came about in something of a rush as the chaotic and cruel purges of government workers got underway in the first months of 2025. But, in truth, its genesis has been a long time in the making. Each person I have talked to, each community I have visited, each interaction with editors that I have had over the decade that I have been writing about Donald Trump's impact on the body politic of the United States has helped prepare me to understand this brutal chapter in the long American story.

As with my previous ten books, the process has been something of a collective effort. Many people have contributed ideas along the way, have helped me to locate sources, or have, simply, provided pep talks and sympathetic ears during moments of uncertainty or darkness as this writing journey progressed.

I am fortunate beyond measure to have been born into a family that values ideas and prizes the ability to engage in spirited conversation. My parents, Jack and Lenore, and my grandparents — Chimen and

Mimi, Mim and Bob — all helped anchor me in a moral universe in which values mattered more than money and in which empathy was considered an ultimate good. My aunt, Jenny, introduced me to the world of journalism, and to the men and women who peopled it in London during the 1980s and 1990s when I was coming of age. My siblings, Kolya and Tanya, have always provided succor during both the good times and the bad. Theirs are voices of wisdom and compassion that help guide me along the byways of life. My cousins, Lauren, Rob, Maia, Nick, and Emma have, over the years, helped nurture and preserve family memories.

My children, Sofia and Leo, are beacons of light in a sometimes bleak world, keeping me on the straight and narrow and always providing me reasons to search for optimism amidst the gloom. I love them more than I can express, and I am quite simply overjoyed to watch them as they spread their wings and start their lives as young, compassionate, and fiercely independent adults.

My wife, Marissa Ventura, never fails to bring into our home joy and laughter, or to remind me that perspective is important — and that sometimes the ultimate goal isn't to work eighteen hours in the day. I count my blessings every day to have found love and joy and even some frivolity again in middle age.

A bevy of colleagues and friends, the members of which are too numerous to mention each and every one by name, have also contributed their interpretations and ideas along the way. To you all, a collective yawp of appreciation.

But there are some whom I must give special thanks to by name for their words of wisdom and their support — financial, intellectual, and otherwise — over the decades. My mentor from Oxford days, Andrew Graham, has been a perennial enthusiast for my journalistic interpretations of the world, as has been my Columbia University Graduate School of Journalism mentor, Sam Freedman. Both of you are, to my mind, modern-day incarnations of Socrates, your exceptional and didactic teaching methods honed to stimulate thought and discussion. My agent, Victoria Skurnick, has always backed my work up with a keen eye and a valuable critical voice. My editors at *The Nation* over the years, including Victor Navasky, Katrina vanden Heuvel, Don Guttenplan, Roane Carey, Lizzy Ratner, Christopher Shay, Shuja Haider, and Regina Mahone, have been instrumental in helping me frame and focus my ideas, as has been Bhaskar Sunkara, current president of the magazine, and as was Christopher Hitchens — whom I was privileged to intern for as a young journalist back in the mid-1990s. My fellow columnists and writers at *The Nation*, including Elie Mystal, Joan Walsh, John Nichols, Jeet Heer, Chris Lehmann, and Katha Pollitt have provided the sort of brains trust a writer usually can only dream of.

At the University of California at Davis, my colleagues in the writing program and the writing center have, over decades, provided intellectual friendship and moral camaraderie. To you all, a special doffing of the cap in gratitude. So, too, I am infinitely grateful to the generations of students I have taught, some of whom have continued on into the world of professional writing, many of whom have given me ongoing appreciation for how young people engage, in ever-new ways, with the world of ideas.

Spread around the world, my friends from childhood and university and journalism, as well as those simply accumulated during the normal course of things, have talked ideas with me, broken bread with me, argued and discussed with me over drinks late into the night, and generally helped me find places to anchor in a storm-tossed world.

Special thanks to Eyal Press, Adam Shatz, George Lerner, Carolyn Juris, David Yaseen, Maura McDermott, Kim Gilmore, to my ex-wife Julie Sze, to Theo Emery, Audie Cornish, Eric Klinenberg, Jason Ziedenberg, Jerry Singleton, Elana Zilberg, Steve Magagnini, Vicki Colliver, Jennifer Packer, Kimberly Winston, Joe Rubin, Glenn Backes, Shawn Hubler, Holly Cooper, Jessica Bartholow, Teven Laxer, Lara Downes, Gina Neff, Gina Ayon, Eric Baliantz, Bruce Haynes and Simon Sadler. To Anders Krab-Johansen, Andrew Cooper, Sameera Khan, and to Jesse Moss, Amanda McBaine, and Andrew Moss. Thanks, too, to Jon Wedderburn, Ben Caplin, and Clive Swillman, amongst my oldest and dearest of friends, and to Jonathan Freedland for his insights, from afar, into US politics. To my PPE crew from Oxford days — Jim Driscoll, Kitty Ussher, Kate Raworth, Kitty Stewart, Tim Kelsall, Tim Johnson, Matt Cavanaugh, Charlotte Cool, Christina Boswell, and the other members of our informal brains trust. Our reunion dinners in gastro pubs in London never fail to stimulate new thoughts. To Pete Sarris, for always-fascinating lunch meetings at The Athenaeum. To Roman Krznaric, for his extraordinary philosophical and historical insights — and his ability to engage in discussions of tennis trivia with me when politics gets too overwhelming. And to Jon Cohen and Shannon Bradley, amongst my newer of friends, but no less important for that; your dinner party and the people you introduced me to around your dining room table back in early 2025 provided a much-needed starting point for this book.

Financially, the reporting for this book was made possible in part by a fellowship from the Type Media Center. For that support, and for the confidence the center's staff expressed in this project, I am most appreciative.

I could all too easily continue this list for many more pages, but would, I suspect, try the patience of my readers. Suffice it to say that I have been blessed to have a large, and intellectually panoramic, network of relatives, friends, colleagues, and experts from miscellaneous fields, to call on over the years, as well as funders who have, at various key moments in my career, provided the backing I needed to develop my projects in depth. This book is the product of all of that collective wisdom and support. To all of you who have made me who I am and helped shape what I believe in, who have molded how I work and made possible what I publish, I am infinitely grateful.

Sasha Abramsky is *The Nation*'s Western correspondent and the author of a weekly political column for the magazine. His work has also appeared in *The Atlantic, The New Yorker Online, The New Republic, The Village Voice, The Guardian, Rolling Stone,* and many other publications. He is the author of eleven books, including *The American Way of Poverty: How the Other Half Still Lives, The House of Twenty Thousand Books, Little Wonder: The Fabulous Story of Lottie Dod, the World's First Female Sports Superstar,* and *Chaos Comes Calling: The Battle Against the Far-Right Takeover of Small-Town America.* Abramsky teaches writing at UC Davis. Follow him on Bluesky at @sashaabramsky.bsky.social.